LIFE CHANCES

Ralf Dahrendorf
LIFE CHANCES

Approaches to Social and Political Theory

WEIDENFELD AND NICOLSON · LONDON

Weidenfeld and Nicolson
91 Clapham High Street London SW4

ISBN 0 297 77682 7

Printed by Willmer Brothers Limited
Rock Ferry Birkenhead Merseyside

Contents

Preface

The subject of this volume is simple: what are human societies about? Yet no one will be surprised to learn that the simplicity of the subject is deceptive. If the question could be answered in one sentence, there would be no need to write a book about it; and if there was a definitive answer to it, there would not be a library of publications on the subject. The search for a substantive definition of the social process takes us to the busy crossroads of theoretical social science, philosophy of history, and political theory. There is no reason to apologize for these much abused concepts, for all three describe respectable concerns which we shall approach in this volume from a variety of angles.

It is not my intention to become autobiographical here, nor do I want to claim harmony for the incompatible by making too many 'on the one hand – on the other hand' statements; but perhaps it is appropriate to premise the substantive argument by a comment on the question of where the threads of this argument are joined for its author.

Much of my work on theoretical social science was published some two decades ago. The book on *Class and Class Conflict* has given rise to considerable debate. Some essays on the same subject have been reprinted and quoted repeatedly. Nevertheless I have always been aware of the fundamental insufficiency of these approaches – not so much because they sought strictly theoretical statements, informed as they were by Popper's extreme rigour, and in the process occasionally lost colour and warmth, and that means above all they lost the dimension of history; rather because even within their self-imposed restrictions they did not go far enough. It may be that the demand for strict theory in the social sciences amounts in the end to a virtual prohibition of knowledge, and that those who do not want to settle for the trivial should both bear Popper in mind and forget his strictures in their work. Even so, theory need not be as formal, as far removed from substantive concerns, from the real motives of men and the specific subjects of historical battles, as it has long been for me. This volume is an attempt to overcome the formalism of my early theoretical approaches and thus to prepare the ground for new theoretical developments.

This has been helped by experiences which in the nature of the case could not remain formal. There was, to be sure, a phase even in my political activity – that of the 'change of power' in Germany in 1969 when after twenty years of Christian Democratic rule a centre-left government under Willy Brandt came into office – in which change as such, 'movement for movement's sake', had become the issue; and some of my critics may not find it an accident that my own commitment was strongest at this point. But in the practical world the demand for change for its own sake does not take one very far. The exaggeration of an almost contentless notion of reforms in the 1960s, and the subsequent equally contentless aversion against reforms in the 1970s tells the story. One has to know what one wants, and what is more, one can know it. This requires, however, an effort of reflection which transcends the merely constitutional, and is not content with making the case for the rules of the game of democracy or their change.

For me, the search for substantive definitions of the social process is linked, from both the theoretical and the practical perspectives, with the idea of liberty, and with the political force of liberalism. I use the latter term hesitantly, however often it may appear in this volume. Liberal parties exist in almost every conceivable political configuration, from the social-democratic position of the Canadian to the conservative position of the Australian Liberals, with some young Liberals in Britain and Germany on the left wing, and some old Liberals in Italy and Holland on the right wing. Strictly speaking, I am not concerned with any of these positions. On the other hand, I would not wish to add to the critique of what has come to be called 'really existing socialism' that of really existing liberalism; I do not expect from reality that it reproduces the purity in a suburb of Minneapolis was in no relevant sense 'there' in Tacitus's Germans or in the men whose skulls anthropologists have recently assembled in Tanzania; and space travel is not simply the extension of the horse and carriage. To say that new things were possible is not to say that they were *in nuce* present in the old. (The familiar distinctions between modes of possibility are relevant here.[10]) New things are, rather, the result of the creative process of human development. History is the process which results from a succession of inventions of man which are unpredictable in substance as well as in timing.

It is hardly necessary to point to the fact that a cursory analysis of this kind leaves open many more questions than it answers. So far, we have merely discussed the possibility of a human history in which something new occurs. This does not mean that the invariants of the Preacher lose their meaning; nor does it rule out the search for invariant laws of social development. (Popper convincingly says: 'There can be invariant laws *and* emergence; for the system of invariant laws is not sufficiently complete and restrictive to prevent the emergence of new law-like properties.')[11] But this discussion suggests a notion of human development, according to which new possibilities can and perhaps must be explored, because by this process man may grow and advance the substance of human nature itself. The idea of emergence makes it superfluous to try to refute the Preacher or Machiavelli in order to make way for the assertion that a concept of history is plausible which permits progress, that is, the extension of human life chances.

At this point there is a meeting of the two questions, whether there is such a thing as history and whether history has any meaning. Let us nevertheless start again and wonder: What are we asking, if we raise the question of the meaning of history?

'History has no meaning,' says Karl Popper, but adds a little later: 'Although history has no meaning, we can give it meaning.'[12] If this is merely to say that history is a concept and not a *Ding an sich*, we have dealt with it, and it is of limited interest.

But Popper would not be content. His scepticism goes further, and it is both justified and dangerous.

First, it is justified. Popper's vitriol throughout the great critique called *The Open Society and its Enemies* is poured over those who claim that they have traced The Path, that is, the course of history as one which has a built-in meaning. Hegel, for instance, claims with characteristic pomp (though without circumstance) that after his excursions through the Oriental, the Greek and the Roman empires, the spirit comprehends 'in the extreme of his absolute negativity, the turning point which is in and for itself, the infinite positivity of this inside of his, the principle of the unity of divine and human nature, the reconciliation as the objective truth and liberty appearing within the consciousness of self and subjectivity, which the Nordic principle of the Germanic peoples has been charged to implement'.[13] It is only too easy to make fun of Hegel; his work shows clearly how much the profession of seers has deteriorated since Kalchas the son of Thestor. Beyond mirth, however, there remains in Hegel's philosophy of history – as in that of all his successors to the Right as well as the Left – a claim that the schedule of history is in itself the unfolding of a process of meaning: that ultimate arrogance of the mind which responds to Kant's worrying question about the function and place of earlier generations by declaring them mere stepping stones on the road to Nordic perfection, or at least to the eve of the great revolution. The evidence for such discoveries of The Path is lacking, and the moral implications of the assumption are dubious: after Popper, the poverty of historicism hardly needs further discussion. In asking for the meaning of history, we are definitely not asking for a schedule of events which is in itself the unfolding of a master plan, divine, world-spiritual, or otherwise.

But Popper makes a risky jump from this conclusion to an activism which is as well-meaning as it is unfounded. Walter Schulz reflects current wisdom when he says: 'Not only a possible answer, but the very *question* of an absolute and ultimate meaning of history has become irrelevant (*inaktuell*).'[14] What then are we to do instead? 'Concrete practice' must take the place of 'abstract theory'. We have quoted Marx's Eleventh Thesis on Feuerbach already. This approach, however well-intentioned it may be, is full of pitfalls. The *trahison des clercs*, the treason of the intellectuals, is one of the great sins of our time, and of its philosophers in particular. Was it not Martin Heidegger who told his students in his Rectorial Address of 1933 that the time had come for the *Lehrstand*, the scholars, to stand back and relinquish the ground to the *Wehrstand*, the militia of the storm troopers? This is what can happen if philosophers cease to interpret the world and call for action instead.

Moral consequences apart, the jump from an absolute and ultimate meaning of the path of history to concrete practice is intellectually unsatisfactory. There is a gap, and it can be filled. There are at least two ways in which we can ask for the meaning of history without lapsing either into historicism or into blind praxis. One is Kant's approach. Kant assumes certain capacities in men which may or may not be developed. On balance, he finds it difficult not to believe that they will in the end be developed, because he considers the absence of meaning an unbearable idea. However, there is no assumption of a linear process, or even of a path of events; there is only an analysis of how things would happen if they were to happen. It may well be that Feuerbach, Marx and their Young-Hegelian bedfellows would call Kant a theologian for that reason (after all, Kant says himself, 'one sees: philosophy could have its chiliasm too'[15]); but his cautious, genuinely critical approach provides at least a possibility of asking for the meaning of history without falling into the trap of historicism.

If one is still not satisfied with this approach, there remains the other possibility of arguing, so to speak, with Kant against Kant. For by assuming an 'intention of nature' (*Naturabsicht*) which unfolds in history, he has after all put man on a tether, even if he is not led along a predetermined path by remote control. The questions which we want to ask out of concern with this implication are: Is it conceivable that in the process of historical development men create new patterns, opportunities and perspectives? What follows if we try to judge such discoveries by certain explicit ('moral') standards? It may be that the very questions contain a disconcerting claim; but in putting them in this way we avoid not only the historicist fallacy as well as any form of *trahison des clercs*, but also any (tautological?) restriction of the potential of history as is implied by the assumption of human capacities which are embedded in man from the outset.

We would claim no more than verisimilitude for the image of history which arises from such considerations; this may justify the somewhat poetic phrases in which we describe it. The idea which we are pursuing regards human history as a process which is essentially open. It is not predetermined by a schedule of the world spirit or by the hand of God, nor is it merely the ever new combination of ever old elements, nor is it restricted by a given set of human capacities. Not only do we not know what will be tomorrow because we are living in a horizon of fundamental uncertainty, but it is possible that there will be things tomorrow which cannot even be thought today, because they are entirely new – inventions, discoveries, emergent innovations. Thus the crucial element of human existence is not nausea about the eternal return of the same things, but restlessness in view of the permanent possibility of new things. Concerning human nature, there is but one assumption which we need to make, that is, man's creative capacity, the ability to invent and discover, the talent to be not only medium, but agent and author of innovation.

It follows from such assumptions that history does not *have* a meaning either *a priori* or *a posteriori*: we must give it a meaning, if we wish to do so (and we must wish to do so, because the question arises inescapably). But giving history meaning is more than the demand for action; it is a theoretical task, though one of normative theory. What follows (we have asked) if we try to judge discoveries by certain explicit ('moral') standards? Once again, we shall confine ourselves to a few constructive suggestions without securing them in all directions.

Emergence is an empty concept so far as the substance of what is invented or created is concerned. A poem, certainly; a spaceship, perhaps; a method of economic policy, possibly; all these are emergent innovations of history. We shall argue in this volume that among these manifold contents one might prove particularly fruitful for understanding human history, that is, life chances. The concept will be defined a little later. Life chances are the moulds of human life in society; their shape determines how and how far people can unfold. Where there is universal suffrage, they can take part in making political decisions; where *per capita* real income is $10,000 per year, they can afford holidays in Mallorca; where there is unconstrained communication, they can voluntarily establish and develop ties to others; where there is co-determination they can turn mere membership of an organization into participation in running it. The specific combination of options and ligatures, of choices and linkages, which makes up human life chances in society is also the material which is moulded and shaped in history and thus provides the subject matter of judgments about the meaning of history.

The important point, however, is not that life chances are the subject matter of history, but that there can be new life chances in the strict sense of the word. The discovery of America has opened up new life chances, as has the invention of the printing press, the reformation of Christianity by Luther and Calvin, and the Copernican transformation of our experience of the earth, the sun and the universe. (Whether it was an 'axis time' or not, the turn of the fifteenth to the sixteenth century was richer in innovations than almost any other known period; even though one might make similar claims for the discovery of mind in ancient Greece or the first settlement of nomads.) New life chances have meaning for people; possibly not for all, at any rate not immediately, and thus at first for only a few; but meaning begins at certain points and then spreads – which is in itself an important historical process.

It is not easy to describe the meaning of new life chances.

The words which come to mind all stem from an organic vocabulary which implies capacities and abilities that are alien to an open understanding of history: people unfold; they grow; they mature; they realize themselves. That people (can) grow is a beautiful expression; though we have to bear in mind that such growth is more than the opening of the seed corn, the breakthrough of the first shoots, their unfolding and blossoming, maturity and death; rather, it is a continuing and permanently incomplete process, a process moreover in which mutations take place and ever new stages of maturity are reached the seeds of which create new starting points which differ in shape from those which had determined their own origins. Piltdown man and members of the *Académie Française* are in no relevant sense 'the same', and it is a debating point whether Pericles and Helmut Schmidt are, or rather (to avoid the irony of irrelevancies) whether the average citizen of Athens in the fourth century BC was φύσει, that is in terms of human nature, in any sense the same as the average citizen of Hamburg in the twentieth century AD.

If there is anything in these reflections, they suggest at least a possible meaning of history – to create more life chances for more people. There is the familiar process of extending given life chances; its limits are defined, and it does not strictly involve innovation. The invention of new life chances, on the other hand, remains a mysterious process which can only very partly be brought about by deliberate action. (Both will concern us further.) Thus it is not easy to tell what the demand for more life chances for more people means in practice. (Although here also clear answers are possible for given historical situations.) What can be defined, however, is the ideal result, that is, the extension of human nature into ever new possibilities of activity, in which options are linked with ties or ligatures.

This conclusion, however, merely rephrases our initial question without answering it: Is the permanent extension of human life chances desirable? And if this is so, why? Hegel praised Plato as the first great mind who realized the principle: 'What is reasonable that is real; and what is real, that is reasonable.'[16] However close they were, both Plato and Hegel were in one respect only too transparently ideologists of their times. Hegel's proposition is a prison without escape, a prohibition of anything new, the forever closed gate of history. It has been said of Marx that all he did was to replace the 'is' in Hegel's proposition by a 'will be'; but this does not improve matters. It merely means that the gates will be closed tomorrow (which is exactly what has happened in countries which applied Marx). Kant comes much nearer to the notion which we have in mind, although his term, 'intention of nature', is somewhat bothersome. It is hard to think that what is possible should not become real. Possibility is both hope and quest. Whoever rejects both may dream of an Arcadian shepherd's life, but will in fact find himself in the position of sheep which desperately seek, in the rocky desert of the Jordan, something to feed on, and would in any case 'not fill the emptiness of creation with respect to its purpose as reasonable nature.'[17]

Thus these approaches to social and political theory are based on a decision. Human life chances can be extended; people can grow in response to their life chances. One measure of the historical process is the extent to which this actually happens. Human societies gain their quality by their ability to offer more people more life chances. Individuals render their contribution to a meaningful process of history by inventing, realizing and extending life chances. History is a journey to ever new river banks and ocean beaches – but this must not be misunderstood: it is not only the alternatives and options, thus the ever *new* things that matter, but the banks and beaches, the ties and linkages as well.

In his *Idea Towards a General History With Cosmopolitan Intent*, to which we have already referred repeatedly, Kant links consideration of the moral consequences (the 'pragmatic implication') of human nature with references to the manner in which the historical process progresses. 'The means which nature uses in order to bring about the development of all its capacities' – we would say, the means which man uses by virtue of his creative nature in order to bring about more life chances for more people – is the antagonism of these within society, insofar as this becomes in the end the cause of their lawful order. I understand by antagonism in this context the unsociable sociability of man, that is, his inclination to enter into society which is at the same time accompanied by a persistent resistance which permanently threatens to disrupt this society.'[18] The quotation must suffice here as an indication; the theory of social change by conflict is not our subject. Otherwise it would have to be shown that the potential of life chances in given societies is often greater than existing structures permit, both as far as hitherto unknown life chances are concerned and with respect to the extension of those already known; that this contradiction finds its expression in social conflicts, in which certain groups act in the name of potential chances whereas others see their interests satisfied in prevailing structures; that such conflicts lead to changes, that is, to the realization of new potential life chances all the time, though the rhythm of change may vary; that occasionally (though not necessarily dramatically) more radical changes take place, changes of subject or theme, by which new dimensions of human life chances are introduced into the process of history; and that in applying it to real societies a model of this kind would have to take account of the many faultings of reality. But, to repeat the point, we shall not pursue here the social theory of change.

On this matter, however, there is an impression which definitely has to be corrected at this stage, namely, that progress is inevitable and in that sense there is a path of history after all. There is no basis for this assumption, and nothing that has been said here was meant to suggest it. So far as the issue of progress is concerned, our somewhat aphoristic discussion of the question of the meaning of history was meant to make one point only: that progress is possible. Is it also real? Here, we shall do no more than take a few cautious steps into the jungle of the concept of progress, a strange concept, which when it was first used was specific and harmless, then became abstract has narrow limits. What it is meant to illustrate, however, may still be valid. It might well be that there are certain basic human experiences which do, or at least appear to, repeat themselves under varied circumstances, but that at the same time these circumstances are more than combinations and permutations of identical elements; they make sense only if we look at them in terms of a process of change. There are certain approaches of the mind which focus on invariant phenomena and reactions, such as religion, and there are others which concentrate on the process of change, such as history, or social science; both have to be seen in conjunction if we want to understand the human condition.

If this kind of consideration tells us no more than that history is possible, then the second answer aims at understanding what history is made of. The concept which is crucial here is that of *emergence,* that is, the appearance of new things. Karl Popper has argued impressively (in the book *The Self and Its Brain*) that it makes no sense to try and dispute the emergence of new things. 'It seems to me to be obviously wrong to say that the faculty of writing poetry existed, *in nuce*, in the lemur.'[8] What is peculiar about man is his creative potential, his ability to introduce into the process of development new things which have never been there before. 'The idea of "creative" or "emergent" evolution . . . is very simple, if somewhat vague. It refers to the fact that in the course of evolution new facts and things occur, with unexpected and indeed unpredictable properties; things and events that are new, more or less in the sense in which a great work of art may be described as new.'[9] Popper's description of natural evolution from 'hydrogen and helium' to 'World 3' of the mind is to be understood not as a sequence of necessary stages of a predetermined process, but as an *ex post* systematization of emergent evolution.

For this is crucial about the idea of emergence: the process of human development consists neither of ever new combinations of the same elements nor is it the mere unfolding of capacities which were there from the outset. (This too would be a version of 'nothing new under the sun'.) The well-to-do two-car family is no new thing under the sun.'[7] The Preacher is not alone in holding this view. Incest and adultery, sickness and suffering, even love and happiness were present in Egypt (or almost anywhere else for that matter) at all times, says the writer; and he is concerned with these eternal fundamentals of life. The politician may find other things fundamental, but if he has read his Machiavelli he will say much the same about power and obedience, war and peace. And many a philosopher will follow, or perhaps precede them and argue that progress is but a figment of the mind, that movement is there for movement's sake, that the depth structure of things will never change, that everything has happened before. Is there then no such thing as history at all?

History is certainly not a thing. It is a concept which we form of the process of actions and events in which human beings were involved. (Though its aspects are not irrelevant, we shall leave natural history out of consideration.) This, however, is little more than a nominalist commonplace. The more important questions are whether we can think of ourselves without thinking at the same time of a process which links us with our forefathers, and (more modestly perhaps, though in the end more convincingly) whether history is not at least conceivable as a process which is more than the unending repetition of the same. Let us leave the former, psycho-philosophical question on one side and concentrate on the latter. Two answers are of importance here.

The first is that there is no reasonable argument for inferring from the eternal return of the same in some respects that the same will have to return forever in all respects. It is quite conceivable that the Preacher was right and that there is still something new under the sun. Morning and night are always morning and night, and yet there is Saturday night and Monday night with their very different connotations, there is the long summer night and the early nightfall in winter; there is the evening of first love and the evening of life. This one may still regard in terms of long and involved rhythms which, while they complicate sameness, do not remove it; thus the example question, like coping with sickness, or falling in love, or using discretion in the exercise of power. We encounter questions and we have to give answers, with cruel necessity. The punk rocker or drug addict may decide that his or her life only matters for five wild years or so, and that they do not care about before or after; but this too is an answer to the question of life and its meaning, and perhaps by implication to that of the meaning of history. Social space ('society') and social time ('history') may be categories of reason like 'physical' space and 'physical' time, but they are equally indispensable for defining identity. If a sense of identity, of knowing who one is, is an indispensable prerequisite of life and thus a condition of survival, then making sense of history is a question which has to be answered.

There are not many such coincidences of problems and questions, though there are some, notably at the boundaries of psychology. Also, one must not be misled by the coincidence. Solving the problem is not the same as answering the question. While we are in some sense engaged in the philosophy of politics, the problem (the question?) of the relationship between philosophy and politics remains. Karl Jaspers has shown that even the great philosophers have sometimes found their solu-tions to problems of little help in answering questions, or at any rate that their biographers find it hard to deny this regrettable circumstance.[6] Many great politicians have found the solution of problems (even if they were proposed by Keynes) quite unhelpful in answering questions. All that is proved by the fact that we are moving along, and at times across, the boundary of problems and questions is that our concern is urgent.

But we must now retrace our steps and look at the problem itself: What, if anything, does it mean if we speak of history? What, if anything, does it mean if we speak of the meaning of history?

'Is there anything whereof it may be said, See, this is new?' When the Preacher put this question, he had in fact answered it already: 'The thing that hath been, it is that which shall be; and that which is done is that which shall be done: and there certain thermodynamic processes? How many patterns of modernization are there? Such questions may still be 'neutral', that is, similar in methodological status to those of the rapidity and radicalness of change. But they also leave the map of change unfastened, like a compass gone wild near the magnetic north pole. The map makes sense only if we answer questions like: What do different patterns of modernization do to people? Does a modern society deserve a plus-sign or a minus-sign in relation to others? (And what labels describe the quality of these 'others'?) Many ways round this question have been sought. When economists talk of 'welfare', the term sounds operational and 'neutral' enough. But on close inspection it is not, and economists know it: 'A complete welfare function is also a value standard which permits the judgment whether and to what extent a factual or possible situation is "better" than another and constitutes "progress" in relation to the total cluster of goals. One is concerned with no more and no less than a practically applicable definition of what we mean when we use the word "progress".'[5] The quotation marks cannot deceive us about the central point that analysis of the direction of social change has to be fastened somewhere in a space which allows judgments about things being better and worse, about progress and regress. As we ask where social change is leading, we cannot evade the notion of historical context, and of the value relationship between various historical processes.

All this, however, is still the *problem* of history, that is, the scientific concern with the direction of social processes. Unlike *questions*, problems can remain unsolved. It does not matter in real life whether they are solved or not, and not solving them is not another way of solving them. Who cares about the theory of social change? The social scientist perhaps, or some social scientists; but even they need not lose any sleep over having left a problem or two open. (Science is about problems, and thus about a 'non-Euclidean' world with its own rules. The question may be asked therefore: Is science necessary? We shall try to answer this when we consider 'representative activities' in the final chapter.) But making sense of history also raises a

BBC sent a group of city-dwellers to live in a phoney iron-age village as human material for a film, the producer found one day that his iron-agers had secretly escaped to Bournemouth because they craved fish and chips. The new barbarism is as popular as, if not the iron age, then some variant of Rousseau. It befits a society which tries desperately, and vainly, to transform 'positional goods' into 'material goods';[2] but it does not befit a tract which is concerned with the progress of liberty.

Thus we are left with the somewhat bold attempt to deal with a large subject in an elliptic, allusive manner – for those who either know, or know that they do not know.

Asking for the meaning of history is unfashionable, if not impermissible. Too many have tried to make sense of history, and it does not seem to have made much difference. 'Philosophers have merely interpreted the world differently; what matters is, to change it.'[3] Needless to say, we do not share such masochism. Thoughtless action is much worse than inconsequential interpretation. But the doubt cannot be dismissed as to whether the question of the meaning of history has itself any meaning. We shall entertain this doubt presently.

But let us bypass it first and argue that the subject is in fact inescapable. This is not said lightly. Making sense of history is one of those concerns of man which respond to *problems* and to *questions* at one and the same time.[4] Problems are man-made, notably scientist-made. For the social scientist, it is important to find out, by measurement or *Verstehen* or by any other tool at his disposal, how societies change: how rapidly? how radically? and above all, in what direction? Of these three (there may be others), the dimension of direction is special in that it transcends formal (value-free?) analysis. What kind of map enables us to determine the direction of social development? There are of course 'neutral', quantifiable answers, such as population growth or decline, urbanization, crime rates, levels of savings and investment, and so on. Such scattered information is of limited use. We may put it together into clusters which describe a more general trend, say, modernization. Questions remain: Is modernization irreversible, like

1 Anything New Under the Sun?

On the Meaning of History and the Possibility of Progress

How can we make sense of history? What is the meaning of man's march through time? This is a large question and also an unfashionable (some would say, an impermissible) question. Yet it is a necessary one. Let us consider the three attributes of this question, before we try to make the case that progress is possible, even though its reality remains precarious.

Large questions leave the European at the end of the twentieth century with a difficult choice: he is an epigone. Somewhere inside the mountain of secondary writings about any large subject there is a mass of primary thought, crystallized or still volcanic. (That this is so proves the fact of history, if nothing else.) It is a paper mountain of course, with ideas pressed into indistinct packages, or flying about in scraps, or hidden in sheets under sheets under sheets. One way of dealing with it is to try and take stock of the lot. Who was it who first tried to make sense of history? Herakleitos? The folk and country singers of the great myths of the Mediterranean or the Himalayas? It was seers anyway, inspired individuals such as 'Kalchas, the son of Thestor, and most excellent of seers, who knew the present, the future and the past'.[1] But the attempt to take stock is not only doomed to failure for its sheer magnitude, it is also more admirable than useful, impressive in an abstract sense without impressing anyone. We shall avoid such useless erudition. This is not a history of thought on history.

On the other hand, we shall also avoid the new barbarism which says that since there is too much to know one may as well ignore the lot. Apart from everything else, there is something contrived and implausible about this attitude. When the

of the ideal; quite apart from the fact that the liberal rarely needs to be ashamed of the realities created in his name as the socialist has to be much of the time. Still, in this respect, there remain ambiguities in the chapters of this volume, though they are such that the author finds it quite possible to live with them happily, and the reader may be able to tolerate them as well.

Such asides must not be misunderstood: this is not a political, but a theoretical book. It aims at understanding, not at change. Nor does it yield to the illusion that theory is already practice. The very fact that it aims at understanding may also make the somewhat unsystematic character of the volume excusable.

Throughout we pursue, in a plurality of approaches, the same set of questions: how can more people come to enjoy more life chances? And what does it mean if one formulates the objective of social processes, of historical change and political activity, in this manner? Here and there (though rarely), the various approaches may overlap; they emerge from different starting points and do not form a totally integrated whole. This does not seem inappropriate to me. Large subjects are best approached in small steps. So far as I am concerned, the time of comprehensive treatises is over; they are replaced by encyclopaedias where completeness is intended, and by essays, where the point is exploration at the risky frontiers of knowledge.

Theory is more than analysis and yet it is its servant. Every now and again there shines through the reflections of this volume a deeper analysis of the contradictions of modern society and the potential of change which they contain. This is my next subject, and the present volume offers a few tools and indications towards it.

London, January 1979   R.D.

and quite explosive, only to be put aside with embarrassment by many today.

Reinhard Koselleck has described the late discovery and quick bloom of 'progress as a category of movement which indicates an historically irreversible climb to the better'.[19] When this bloom reached its climax in the decades before and after the more-or-less revolutions of 1848, even Marx and Engels had no more than mild reservations about the fashionable concept: 'One realizes that progress is the essence of mankind, but one does not have the courage to proclaim progress openly.'[20] 'In fact there is nothing in history which does not serve human progress in one way or another, though often by an immense detour.'[21] Kant of course had answered the question of 'whether mankind is permanently progressing to the better' half a century earlier by distinguishing between a 'regulatory' and a 'constituent' concept of progress; the latter and dubious one regards progress as a constituent feature of human history, whereas the former measures varied realities in terms of moral rules and thus recognizes progress as well as regress.

It is hardly necessary to state that we are concerned exclusively with the regulatory concept of progress. Even the compromise which began with the competitions of eighteenth-century academies about morals and technology, and finds its modern expression in a statement by Daniel Bell, yields little: 'We can make more and more things: we do not change nature. There is in social structure (the techno-economic order) a principle of linear change and cumulation. . . . But in culture there is no cumulation, but rather a *ricorso* to the primordial questions which confront all men in all times and places. . . . The principle of culture is thus that of a constant returning – not in its forms, but in its concerns – to the essential modalities that derive from the finitude of human existence.'[22] I do not share this view. Clearly, the finitude of human existence is a constant, and the virtue of humility has its foundation in it. (Could it not be, incidentally, that the existential questions of man change their complexion as human nature changes?)

Moreover, it may be that there is a degree of continuity in technical development, though this is hardly linear. (Is it not conceivable, incidentally, that technical development changes its significance dramatically under different conditions of human society?) But then there are life chances – neither an existential constant nor a technological variable – and it is their development on which we want to focus here. And there is liberty, on which so much depends and about which a word has to be said in this context.

There may be a case for cutting through the tangle of 'ifs' and 'perhapses' and stating three propositions of which it can be shown that they are at least plausible: Progress is possible. The progress of man's potential is real. Some progress of human life chances is probable.

Progress is possible. At first sight, this proposition seems unobjectionable enough, almost obvious. There is, of course, the matter of definition: progress of what? But when we speak of progress, we mean that of human life chances. They can be enhanced and extended; new life chances can emerge as a mould for new patterns of human nature. On second sight, the seemingly innocuous proposition reveals its problems. By saying that progress is (merely) possible, we imply that regress is possible also. Under no circumstances will we state or imply that progress is necessary; it is precarious even when it is real. Men may define objectives of their historical struggles, but we cannot know of any destination to which man inevitably progresses. Another implication is more difficult still; we shall leave it unanswered here. By saying that progress of life chances is possible we imply that new sets of life chances emerging in real societies do not cancel out and destroy those that were there before; change is potentially more than change from one evil, or even one good, to the other. But is this true? Are not the gains of hierarchy irretrievably lost in modernity? Must not a new theme inevitably destroy the gains of modernity with its deficiencies?

The progress of man's potential is real. The word potential may mean several things, and it is time to distinguish and clarify.

In one sense, man's capacities can be called his potential; they are faculties, dispositions which can be developed although at a given moment they are not; this is, if the paradox is permitted, the real potential of individuals, say, their musical talent, or their ability to live with complexity. Then there is a more abstract sense of the word in which we are not talking of the real potential of individuals, but that which is present somewhere in a given society, and which for individuals is often no more than a potential, so to speak. 'If I were a Rockefeller, I could buy a castle on the Loire.' Societies too can have a potential potential, that is, life chances which appear somewhere in their structure without being general. Who has not wished to combine the attractions of city life with the securities of the village? Or even the effects of work with the pleasures of free activity? Finally, there is potential in the sense of mere potential, figment of fantasy, hope for the future, and, for example, man's potential of making contact with neighbours in the universe.

This is a confusing picture, and we shall not try to clarify it to the extent of introducing different terms, if only because there are after all connections between the potentials. At this stage, however, we are not primarily concerned with the real potential of individuals, nor with the mere potential of future worlds. We are arguing, rather, that the real potential of societies is growing, and the case rests on the wisdom of the saying that there is no better proof of possibility than reality.

Many kinds of human life chances have been real somewhere, sometime. As we travel into the past, we often seek to find traces of the life chances of another age, the historian in the archives, the archaeologist on his site, the anthropologist in his field, and the tourist in Machu Pichu and Fatehpur Sikri. To be sure, there was a price. Not every young Athenian strolled through the halls of the academy to philosophize in a leisurely manner about God and the world; building the seven wonders of the world killed more people than they pleased; and the fortunes made by the early Rockefellers and Vanderbilts cost the blood, sweat and tears of many others. But life chances they were, the academy, the wonders of the world, and the early American fortunes; real life chances for some. Our argument is that they all add up to a great mass – no pattern or structure yet, unfortunately – of potential. Everything that has been real at some time is obviously possible, whether man's collective memory preserves it in myth or historiography or not. And given the creativity of man, there is much to choose from – if only everything that was possible could be realized at one and the same time!

One may well argue that this abstract potential of man is of little relevance to real people. (One may even suspect built-in reasons why the entire potential could not possibly be realized at one time.) This makes our third proposition all the more important: Some progress of human life chances is probable.

Modern societies have developed their own strains and contradictions. There is, however, another side of the coin. Many survival problems threatening pre-modern man have been resolved. Economic development has increased human welfare greatly. There is much experience today of the rule of law and political democracy; there are even widespread pressures towards these values. Voluntary mobility has increased considerably. Representative activities are open to more people. Progress is never a one-way street, and it may well be that the dangers accompanying such developments balance their gains. But there does appear to be progress in the total volume of life chances and the number of people to whom they are offered.

This is the progress of modern society. There is, of course, the much wider perspective of 'cosmic evolutionary stages'. There was no poetry in the lemur. We have referred already to the 'discovery of mind' in ancient Greece.[23] From 'sentience' through 'consciousness of life and death' and 'human language' there leads a long road to 'works of art and of science (including technology)' (to quote Popper's analysis of emergent stages once again);[24] and one may well argue that this progress was accompanied if not conditioned by growing life chances.

One could go on amassing illustrations, but they do no more than make the initial proposition plausible. At the very least we shall retain the presumption that some progress of life chances is probable. This is emphatically not a presumption about linear, or any other pattern of progress. It is, by itself, not even a presumption that progress is always, or ever, desirable. But it is a presumption that, apart from being possible, progress actually happens.

There are new things under the sun. One can conceive of a meaning of history if such new things are defined as life chances. Progress is possible, indeed probable. One word is missing in all this, a concept rather, which invokes the most difficult of questions in this context: Is there a progress of liberty?

Man is a deficient creature and needs society. Society offers him safety or survival chances. It also offers him chances of advancement. Whatever may ultimately set this process in motion, it moves forward through the unsociable sociability of man, by the antagonisms which arise from it in society, and by the enhancement of existing potentials as well as the emergence of new ones. In the course of this process man changes. Whether he becomes less deficient may be an open question; the baby born in Palo Alto in 1979 is as little (and perhaps less) able to stand on its own feet as the one born ten thousand years earlier in Neanderthal. But beyond certain natural limitations of his capacities, man is challenged by his own actions to respond to varying, often new and wider chances in his conditions of life. These do not always grow. There are times when the rock rolls back once Sisyphus has pushed it up the hill and tumbles all the way down to the plain in which it started. We do not know whether the rock will ever get to the top, although modern men, contrary to Sisyphus, have built artificial steps half way up the hill beyond which it does not roll back if it gets out of control. There may be progress of life chances, and with respect to the cumulation of possible life chances there is certainly such progress. It is at least conceivable that this results in creating fuller human beings than lived three centuries ago, to say nothing of the stone age.

But this detached and uncertain history of mankind has

meaning for people only insofar as it enlarges liberty. In a certain sense the task of liberty is the same at all times; it is that of the open society. Whether there was a long jump to bring it about or not, the chances of formal liberty have probably not improved. In the other respect the task of liberty may be the same as well, but its substance changes all the time; this task is to extend life chances and seek a new potential. There is no freedom without this search; liberty means that we straddle or shift every hurdle which stands in the way of human development.

Can there be a progress of liberty then? If by such progress we understand not merely the return of Germany or Greece to the rule of law, but progressive changes in the circumstances of human life throughout the centuries, then the idea is peculiar and objectionable. Kant was understandably concerned: 'It continues to remain strange in this: that older generations seem to conduct their painful business merely for the sake of later ones, in order to prepare for them a step from which they might raise the construction further which nature has at its intention; and that only the latest should have the good fortune to live in the structure on which a long line of their forefathers (if without intending to do so) have worked without being able to share themselves in the happiness which they have helped prepare.'[25] But there are things which we cannot understand. Beyond such humility, it may also be a property of the structure in question that no one will ever just live in it without contributing to its perfection.

There may thus be a progress of liberty. There may be societies which give more space than others to the desire of men to reduce unnecessary constraints; there may be more open and more developed societies in which life chances are enhanced and extended further. And since this is so, we must never rest in our quest for advancing the frontiers of freedom.

2 Life Chances

Dimensions of Liberty in Society

Happiness is undoubtedly desirable, but as a social value it has at least three disadvantages. One is that it is elusive.

> *Run after happiness* [says Brecht[1]]
> *But do not run too hard!*
> *For all run after happiness,*
> *Happiness runs elsewhere.*

The Founding Fathers of the United States did not need poetic advice to warn them of being over-ambitious; their protestant ethic sufficed to make them settle for the 'pursuit of happiness'. This, however, is hardly less elusive. Sado-masochism and *anorexia nervosa* apart, people tend to pursue happiness in many strange and different ways, by ascetic discipline and by genial indulgence, by inflating their own importance and by devoting themselves to the needs of others, by the search for truth and the search for change. John Stuart Mill seemed quite clear: 'By happiness is intended pleasure, and the absence of pain; by unhappiness pain, and the privation of pleasure.[2] But the simple fact is that what deprives some of pleasure is a source of pleasure for others, and the absence of pain in the sensations of some does not rule out great pain for others. The pursuit of happiness is elusive, because it has so many routes that it defies social and political generalization.

This, of course, is not a new idea. Aristotle grappled with it and decided that there was true happiness and the mere illusion of it. At the best of times, the practical life (for him) cannot produce εὐδαιμονία, genuine happiness; this is to be found in certain activities of the soul among which those of the philo-

sophical mind, the theoretical life, are unsurpassed in purity
and duration. Aristotle knew of course that philosophical
pleasures were likely to be a very individual experience, though
he spoke of the 'even more beautiful and august [condition] if
entire peoples or political communities reach it'.[3] The notion
of 'public happiness' is not meaningless (though it may mean
something rather different, that is, a social state of tranquil
equilibrium, of total legitimacy); but by and large the claim
that societies should be *made* happy must be suspicious. Thus
the second shortcoming of the social use of the word happiness
is that it smacks of decreed happiness. It is surely no accident
that an official publication of a communist country (the
Czechoslovak Soviet Socialist Republic) describes an imaginary
constitution such that Article 1 ascribes to 'every human
being . . . an undeniable right to happiness during his life', and
then adds in Article 2: 'Human society must guarantee this
right by all available means.'[4] Is it hypersensitive if one suspects
that in the end such a society will see a lot of 'all available
means' and little of happiness?

   Then there is the third and most serious shortcoming of
happiness as a social objective; it is deeply unhistorical. Happiness is a state of mind which was as available, if not to Neanderthal and Peking Men (to avoid a difficult discussion), then to
Aristotle, as it was to St Augustine, Thomas Hobbes and John
Stuart Mill. Unless we assume a growing or shrinking capacity
of men to feel happy, the general level of happiness is not likely
to change much, let alone in a systematic fashion. It is a
response the terms of which remain the same whatever the
conditions are to which it is directed; the thermometer of human
temperament does not change (so to speak) as we move from
the 'axis time' of 500 BC to the eclipse of modernity. This is why
'happiness research' is so useless. George Easterlin's finding (in
his article on the question of whether economic growth im-
proves the human lot)[5] that between 1946 and 1966 there has
been no significant improvement in the level of happiness in the
United States, and no change in the relative happiness levels of
groups at all, tells us as little as George Gallup's finding that

there are 'surprisingly' small differences between the happiness
levels of rich and of poor countries.[6] Unless it is intended to
give a semblance of factual support to the thesis that there is no
such thing as progress, and that therefore we may as well leave
things as they are, all that such research shows is that happiness
is a useless index of human social development. We have to dig
deeper and perhaps on a different lot if we want to find out
where human societies are going.

To be sure, liberal thought had its ahistorical aspects. Traditional liberalism is as insistent on formal rules for all sorts of
social games as it is silent on the social condition of man. To the
present day, great liberals have been liable to fall victim to an
almost cynical advocacy of 'movement for movement's sake'
(to quote Hayek), or else, if they were less cynical (like Popper),
to an odd combination of ahistorical formalism and the unfounded demand for acts of moral greatness.[7] Lionel Trilling is
thus both right and involuntarily ambiguous when he states
about liberalism that 'the word happiness stands at the very
centre of its thought.'[8] For this should not be so. Of course, the
defender of freedom, or liberty (and we shall not pursue conceivable distinctions between the two), seeks to achieve an
objective of social and political action which is designed to
benefit individuals above all, and in that sense to create conditions of possible happiness. But he recognizes also the delightful
manifold of human wishes and wants and ways which forbids
even a general definition of happiness; he sees the dangers of
societies which are trying to create, or even guarantee, happiness for all and are quite likely to make more people unhappy
than those which concentrate on more properly social objectives; and he knows of the need for men, in the uncertain
condition in which they live, to try to improve themselves, to
grow, rather than to settle for the pleasure which they can have
here and now. The notion which we need in order to define the
social and political objectives of an active liberalism is one
which anchors opportunities of human growth in patterns of
social structure without overlooking the desirability of personal
satisfaction. We need a genuinely social, and that means of

B

necessity historical, concept of what the process of human societies is about, and one which enables us to give substance both to social theories of change and to the political theory of liberty.

This, too, is not exactly a new objective, and before we explore a constructive answer, two other concepts must be mentioned briefly: utility and welfare. W. L. Davidson has actually linked them with happiness in a rather telling manner: 'Utility, then, is welfare, and welfare covers every conceivable element that goes to determine and constitute man's happiness.'[9] This is an overstatement which does rather less than justice to the concepts of utility and welfare, though it must be said that Jeremy Bentham was strangely worried about the new term which he tried to introduce, utility. (And twenty-five years after the first publication of the *Principles* he had consequently turned the 'utility principle' into the 'greatest happiness or greatest felicity principle'.) But the point about 'utility' is that it turns attention from the individual sentiment of happiness to its causes, social or otherwise.

Whether Bentham did very well in this is another matter. He lacked the endearing blandness of earlier political economists who had talked unashamedly of 'opulence' as the subject of human progress; nor did he have the methodological subtlety of later economists who, like Pareto, used 'utility' as an apparently value-free concept. (One might call it 'X', says Pareto in §2111 of his *Traité*, and nobody should draw any false conclusions from calling it '*utilité*'; what is meant is simply what people find advantageous.)[10] However, Bentham made his point:

By utility is meant that property in any object, whereby it tends to produce benefit, advantage, pleasure, good, or happiness (all this in the present case comes to the same thing) or (what comes again to the same thing) to prevent the happening of mischief, pain, evil or unhappiness to the party whose interest is considered; if that party be the community in general, then the happiness of the community; if a particular individual, then the happiness of that individual.[11]

Leaving the shortcomings of happiness on one side for the moment (which is admittedly difficult), one can see the advantage of the idea of utility. It is ascribed to 'objects'. It can therefore be measured, which Bentham proceeds to do in rather amusing ways.[12] It can also be compared, and thus increased. Utility is a concept which allows progress, as John Stuart Mill insisted when he formulated the moral precept that the greatest happiness principle in the utilitarian sense must be extended not only to all mankind, but 'so far as the nature of things admits, to the whole sentient creation'.[13]

Yet there is something strangely arbitrary about the relation between the properties of objects and the feelings of men. Hanging in mid-air like the gardens of Semiramis we find objects which give pleasure and others which do not, and a prescription to grow more beautiful flowers while getting rid of all weeds. But what about rights, for example? (And Mill had much to say about them when he wrote *On Liberty*.) Are they to be thought of as objects giving pleasure? What about class relations? Are they objects responsible for 'mischief, pain, evil or unhappiness'? The utilitarian approach leaves out the dimension of social structure, of human opportunities and boundaries as they are provided by the norms and sanctions of society. Utilitarians talk about society in a naively voluntaristic way; their morality thus never reaches the dimensions of the political and the social, and by implication it fails to provide a yardstick for measuring progress in historical reality. Comparisons of utilitarian happiness are painfully superficial and uninformative.

This is where Pareto's version of utility, later developed by Pigou and others into the modern concept of welfare, is a considerable step forward. We are, of course, using the term here in its economic sense, as defined for example by Herbert Giersch:

Welfare is the epitome of objectives which are in fact sought or which should be realized. The precise definition of these objectives and their relative significance in terms of sets of objectives is co-terminous with setting up a function to be maximized. For this we use . . . the expression 'welfare function'. A complete welfare function is also a value standard which permits the judgment whether and to what extent a factual or possible situation is 'better' than another and constitutes 'progress' in relation to the total cluster of goals. One is concerned with no more and no less than a practically applicable definition of what we mean when we use the word 'progress'.[14]

The last sentence may explain why we have quoted Giersch rather than, say, Pigou, or even Dahl and Lindblom. Maximizing the welfare function is indeed a definition of progress which is at the same time social and capable of precise assessment, even measurement. For most practical purposes, welfare is surely a rather persuasive definition of what the social process is about.

But practical purposes are not theoretical purposes; and stating this is more than an abstract quibble. The fundamental weakness of the concept of welfare lies in its very strength: it is an empirical rather than an analytical concept, and it is therefore incapable of being used as either an element of the social theory of change or one of the political theory of freedom. The welfare function tells us at the most whether socio-economic and socio-political processes live up to their own potential, and thus allow comparison with other known conditions, earlier in time or elsewhere in space, but it fails to provide a yardstick for assessing the potential of social processes itself. Put in the crudest terms, it tells us how far others are from American conditions of life, but it cannot conceivably tell us how desirable American conditions are. In a crucial sense, welfare is always a descriptive notion, however complex a syndrome of social indicators is used to measure it; what we need, though, is a theoretical instrument for assessing varying empirical welfare functions.

I can only hint here at the two arguments which justify this conclusion. The first has to do with the ordinal-cardinal dilemma of welfare functions, that is, with the fact that in order to make qualitative comparisons possible, assumptions about relative weight have to be built into the function. It sounds reasonable enough to list, with Dahl and Lindblom, 'seven basic ends of social action': freedom, rationality, democracy, subjective equality, security, progress, appropriate inclusion.[15] But what if new ends are suddenly discovered, say because of the external diseconomies of the old ones? Here, explicit value judgments are necessary, and it is hard to disagree with Lionel Robbins when he says: 'I would be the last to deny the importance of the distinction between purely scientific economic analysis and normative prescription. But for me, at any rate, Welfare Economics has always seemed a very draughty halfway house.'[16] The house is equally draughty, and equally halfway, if we look at the other dilemma, that of subjective and objective criteria of welfare. Naturally, welfare economists want to measure the attainment of the objectives of social action as defined by them. In order to do so, they either have to assume that certain items expressed by objectives indices are in fact desired, or they have to turn these into indices of perceived satisfaction, or they have to mix both (as do the OECD social indicators and most recent attempts to improve them). Either way, however, they remain tied to an existing condition of things, immanent to the system of social organization for which they are invented, liable to be overtaken by new developments, and thus descriptive and empirical rather than analytical and theoretical.

There is more to be said about the important concept of welfare and the social indicators used to measure it, but it is time to take stock. Our argument so far has been mainly negative. The search for a concept which defines objectives of the social process in such a way that it can be built into social theories of change as well as the political theory of liberty has not so far been unduly successful. The greatest happiness of the greatest number may have something to do with a free society, but it leaves us with an elusive, individual and ahistorical concept. Maximizing the welfare function may be highly desirable, but it merely describes what can be done given the assumptions and possibilities of an existing social structure. We are looking for a concept which is social in the sense of avoiding reliance on individual perception or, worse still, decreeing what it should be, which is structural in the sense of tying the desired end not merely to random 'objects' but to patterns of social organization, which in consequence of being social and structural is historical, and which is theoretical in the sense of transcending in principle any one given society and its known potential. I shall argue that the concept of life chances can serve this purpose.

'Life chances' is in the first instance a word, and one with rather pleasant connotations. Politicians like to claim that they are improving people's life chances; and by putting the word 'life' and the word 'chance' together in this way, they suggest that something is going to be done that matters to people, and that opens doors. Life chances are, as it were, the opposite of death traps. Social scientists too tend to use the term loosely. Take T. B. Bottomore, for example, who states that studies have shown 'how strong and pervasive is the influence on individual life chances of the entrenched distinctions of social class';[17] or, similarly, F. Hirsch, who describes the concept of equal opportunity as 'not much less question-begging when applied to education than when applied to life chances in general'.[18] Life chances in both cases are, in a somewhat vague sense, the sum total of opportunities offered to the individual by his society, or by a more specific position occupied in society. The element of generalized opportunity is probably crucial.

Half-way between the word and the concept is Max Weber's use of the notion of chance. I say the notion of chance, because while Weber in fact uses the word 'life chances', this for him has specific and in our context, irrelevant connotations. He speaks of 'the competition of different human types for life chances', and means something like this: 'We shall call "selection" the (latent) struggle for existence of human individuals or types for life chances or chances of survival which takes place without any meaningful intention of conflict: "social selection" insofar as the chances of living people in life, "biological selection" insofar as the chances of survival of genes are concerned.'[19] 'Life' is an emphatic word here, nearer to survival than to the fullness of human opportunities. But in many other places, Weber speaks of social chances in ways which are highly relevant to our discussion: 'economic chances', such as 'market chances', 'chances of acquisition', 'price chances', 'supply chances', but also 'social chances', such as the 'typical chance offered by class position', and indeed 'future chances' including those of rebirth and religious justification.[20] Max Weber never included chances, let alone life chances, in his catalogue of 'basic concepts'; but he might well have done. For him the concept signifies in the first instance a methodological reservation; he is trying to avoid dogmatism. Furthermore, it indicates a characteristic of social structure; while social action is not random, there can never be more than a probability that things will happen as prescribed in norms and guaranteed by sanctions. Above and beyond that, however, Weber uses the notion of chance to indicate opportunities provided by social structure, and it is this usage which we intend to develop.

Let me return for a moment to the word, and to the common experience to which it corresponds. (It is, as we shall presently see, a deceptive experience too.) Money provides life chances. We can do something with it. It has significance whether we use it or not. It offers opportunities, indeed in some sense it is the epitome of opportunity ('there is nothing that dollars can't buy'). The right to move from place to place, or even abroad, is an important life chance even for him who stays put all his life. Universal suffrage is a life chance. Many have praised the life chances of cities – the lights, the theatres, the evening classes, the shops, the jobs to choose from, the area to live in (and everything in the plural). They admit that they do not use them much, but like to know that they are there to be used. Today, some tend to praise the life chances of villages instead – the closeness of human contact, the cleaner air, law and order, opportunities for exercise, leisure, creature comforts. There is in fact a lesson here for the definition of the concept.

Life chances are not attributes of individuals. Individuals have life chances in society; their life chances may make or break them; but their lives are a response to these chances. Life chances are a mould. They may be too big for individuals and challenge them to grow; or they may be too restricted and challenge them to resist. Life chances are opportunities for individual growth, for the realization of talents, wishes and hopes, and these opportunities are provided by social conditions. For any given individual – and in a sense, for social groups, strata, classes – there is a balance of life chances. This is true for total societies too. It could be argued for example that modernization has created unrivalled life chances for many.

But before I pursue this analytical thread, the time has come for a moment of rigour. From these somewhat flowery remarks it might appear that life chances are simply opportunities in the sense of alternatives to choose from. The more of these alternatives a person has (or so one might think), the greater are his possibilities and thus his life chances. This, however, would be a deceptively foreshortened, indeed a mistaken, understanding of the concept which we have in mind. Life chances (as we use the term) are a function of two elements, *options* and *ligatures*. They can vary independently of each other, and it is their specific combination at a given time which constitutes the chances by which the lives of people in society are determined.

The terms are not chosen to obfuscate what is after all a clear and unambiguous meaning; they are no more than *chiffres*. Of the two, that of options is the more easily explained. Options are possibilities of choice, or alternatives of action given in social structure. They are in fact what we have in mind when we speak of opportunities, of directions into which the individual can go (even if these are often prescribed for him by his roles). From the point of view of the individual, options are reasons, indeed needs for choice; thus 'option' and 'choice' are the structural and the personal side of the same coin. Options are structural opportunities for choice, to which individual choices or decisions correspond.

The concept of ligatures sounds more alien at first hearing, though it is crucial for our context. Ligatures are allegiances; one might call them bonds or linkages as well. By virtue of his social positions and roles, the individual is placed into bonds or ligatures. These are often burdened with emotional weight for him which is expressed in the very words used to describe them:

forefathers, home country, community. Perhaps it could be said that as choices are the subjective side of options, so linkages, or bonds, are that of ligatures. Bonds or linkages give meaning to the place which the individual occupies. Throughout, the element of ligatures signifies meaning, the anchoring of persons and their actions, whereas options emphasize the objective and horizon of action. Ligatures create bonds and thus the foundations of action; options require choices and are thus open for the future.

Life chances are a function of options and ligatures. It may be worth looking a little more closely at this statement, for it is to be understood quite strictly. It means for example that there may be optimal relations between the two. A maximum of options is not by itself a maximum of life chances, nor is a minimum of options the only minimum of life chances. Ligatures without options are oppressive, whereas options without bonds are meaningless. Pre-modern societies with their overpowering forces of family, estate or caste, tribe, church, slavery or feudal dependence, were in some ways all linkage and no choice. The social bonds of inescapable statuses dominated most people's lives. Modernization has inevitably meant an extension of choice. What people could do depended largely on where they belonged. But modernization provides choices as often as not by the disruption of linkages. Mobility has come to mean that the family or the village are no longer communities of fate, but increasingly become communities of choice. The money economy generalizes social relations in a way that implies the abandonment of many specific bonds. This has often been described; it is of course the prevailing theme of social analysis from Durkheim and Tönnies to Weber and Parsons. Increasingly, people can do things wherever they belong; the worker can vote Conservative, the old lady wear a mini-skirt, and the villager spend his holidays in Mallorca. What matters here is that the reduction, and ultimately destruction of bonds has been accompanied by, and has perhaps been responsible for, an increase of choices up to a point; but from this point onwards choices begin to lose their meaning because they take place in a social vacuum, or better perhaps, a social desert, in which no known co-ordinates make any direction preferable to any other. It is as if people are presented, in their social lives, with ballot papers on which no names of candidates or parties are entered at all and told to vote for just anybody or anything. There is an optimal balance of options and ligatures which may have been upset in the contemporary world.

The examples must not be misunderstood. Choices or options and bonds or ligatures vary independently of each other; their apparently inverse relation is an empirical rather than a logical condition. In principle they can each be measured; they can grow and shrink. This is more immediately plausible with respect to choices. The process called division of labour is by definition an expansion of the range and variety of options. The process called citizenship spreads options, which were originally available to only a few, to more and more people. Whatever traditional measures of gross national product do not tell us, economic growth, even narrowly defined, has something to do with extending the horizon of choice. One could imagine a grid for the classification of dimensions of choice, and further measures which would make interpersonal, intergroup, inter-societal and intertemporal comparisons possible. (There is a research agenda here which might add an important dimension to the 'social indicators movement'.)

Measuring ligatures, or linkages, is much more difficult. They are the (often bizarre) patterns by which social positions are tied to others in order to provide their incumbents with bonds. Such patterns are railings to which people can cling as they walk into the mist of their social lives, just as they can be barriers too which they encounter in this mist. Speaking of their extent can mean several things. For one thing, the sheer number of linkages or ligatures rises as social differentiation goes ahead; factory discipline was as absent from the Greek *polis* as was nationalism or belief in Jones's 'Peoples' Temple'. But the more sensitive aspect (and I am admittedly exploring here, attempting to challenge further thought and research) is the intensity of social ligatures. While it can easily be shown that structural differentiation extends the field in which social sub-contracts create bonds, it could well be argued that the intensity of linkages, the normative penetration of the social roles of individuals, is subject to one of those processes which go in one direction only, from status to contract, from *Gemeinschaft* to *Gesellschaft*. We shall not make this assumption; indeed it is part and parcel of the approach proposed here that this need not be so; but there are not many examples of the deliberate building, or even involuntary emergence of linkages in societies once the process of rejecting bonds in favour of choices has begun.

It is all the more important to emphasize that it is possible to have both choices and linkages, and that the growth of one does not necessarily mean the decline of the other. What we are aiming at here is of course that most complex of ideals (a version perhaps of that elusive value, public happiness), a liberal society that is not libertine, a structure of authority that is not authoritarian, a social order that is not informed by law-and-order hysteria, thus a world in which choices are more than an invitation for endless *actes gratuites*, and bonds are more than painful restrictions of individual development. The extreme cases are intellectual games; a world in which choice is o and linkage is 1 is an animal world of entirely instinctual behaviour, whereas a world in which choice is 1 and linkage o is Robinson's world in which nothing matters (and not surprisingly the two are not that far apart).[21] Between the extremes we find real societies. But the important point is that working out the relation between options and ligatures is not a zero-sum game. While it sometimes appears today as if every choice is invariably paid for by a loss in linkage, it is in fact possible to increase options without losing ligatures. Different histories of modernization are relevant here, as are different theories of development current today. What is more, the entire system of co-ordinates of options/ligatures can move forward, so that a higher level of both is achieved – a point of central importance for any theory of active liberalism. It is possible to increase life chances not only by seeking an optimal balance of given options and ligatures, but by increasing both. It may indeed be the ultimate task of the active search for freedom to work for such growth in man's potential.

This then is the concept which I propose: life chances are opportunities for individual action arising from the interrelations of options and ligatures. Both options and ligatures are dimensions of social structure, that is, they are given as elements of social roles rather than as random objects of people's will or whim. At any time, there is an optimal relationship between options and ligatures – choices and linkages, or bonds, from the individual's point of view – and thus there is a function of options and ligatures which defines a maximum of life chances. Both options and ligatures, however, can grow as well as shrink, thus life chances are capable of increase and extension. Exploring the conditions of an increase in life chances is the first problem of the social theory of change and the first objective of the political theory of liberty.

Why is this concept superior to happiness, utility, and welfare? In one respect it is not. While there can be happiness research, a Benthamite measure of utility ('intense, long, certain, speedy, fruitful, pure. . . .'), and gross national product measures and social indicators of welfare, we have not taken the concept of life chances far enough to provide operational precision. This, however, may be a mere technical deficiency, not one of principle. In principle, we have here the beginnings of a structural concept, analytical rather than descriptive, not linked to any particular society, yet historical in its quality, equally useful for theoretical social science and for political theory, which enables us to come to grips with what has variously been called the objective or end of the social process, the purpose of society, and might even have some relevance for that forbidden yet endlessly attractive territory, the meaning of history. The only question is: Why should life chances be desirable? Much of the remaining argument in this chapter will be devoted to this question.

Were this a chapter on the analysis of contemporary societies, it would be tempting to make the concept of life chances walk at this stage and see where it takes us. Indeed I cannot resist this temptation altogether, although in yielding we shall bear in mind the intention of linking life chances and liberty in order to argue the normative case which has not yet been made.

The societies called modern have brought an enormous increase in human life chances, greater perhaps than that wrought by any other theme of history. The number and range of options available has been increased, as has the number of people to whom these options are available. The concurrent processes of economic growth, political mobilization, social equality and a culture of enlightenment have had this effect, even where they have been stifled by faultings of old and new, or deliberately perverted by totalitarian power. Everywhere, this process was accompanied by a decreasing intensity of social ligatures, for which money as a generalized medium of exchange, mobility and participation, and insistence on the individual as the unit of social order are examples as well as motive forces. Both processes, those of extending options and of demolishing ligatures, are surely unfinished, whatever obstacles they may have encountered in recent years; but future historians may well decide that in a number of the OECD societies, an optimum of life chances was reached at the beginning of the 1970s.

Since then, it is no longer clear whether such optimal conditions exist anywhere. Every one of the motive forces of modern societies has produced its own contradictions; and at times it appears as if these forces are no longer capable of dealing with their effects. More growth does not remove unemployment, and more equality does not overcome the frustrations of citizenship. Among these contradictions there is one which goes to the core of the social contract itself. It is, in practical terms, the problem of law and order or, in theoretical language, that of anarchy, state and utopia, or perhaps of anomie. (It is highly relevant in this context to remember R. K. Merton's important analysis of what he called the 'strain towards anomie' or 'cultural chaos' in modern society.)[22] I shall deliberately overstate the case and not apologize for it, because the overstatement makes a necessary point. Up to a point, the extension of life chances inevitably meant the reduction of human linkages and bonds. Ligatures had to be severed to enable people to make use of the options offered by modern society. To take the most obvious example, suffrage was as meaningless for the farm labourer dependent on an East Elbian *Junker* as it was for the devout Catholic in an Italian village and indeed for the traditional housewife all over the world. It is only by reducing the intensity of such linkages that choices get any meaning at all. But the reduction of linkages became a self-accelerating and seemingly unstoppable process. It began by extending the importance of achieved social positions but in the end it turned against all ascribed positions, whatever their basis. For some, being a Christian begins to mean not having any distinctive faith; women's liberation begins to mean that there must be no social difference between men and women; 'grey panthers' demand the abolition of old age as children's liberationists have demanded the abolition of childhood. This is not a romantic plea for yesterday's world; few prospects are more frightening than that those might prevail who want to take us back to the alleged virtues of the past and who will in fact land us with all its vices again. But we cannot overlook the fact that the destruction of ligatures in significant parts of some societies has begun to lead to a reduction of complexity which in turn involves a decrease in life chances: the choices themselves disappear which a modern society was meant to offer to all.

Nor is this the whole story. The social contract ends the war of all against all by establishing ligatures, linkages. The demolition of ligatures may first help increase options; it certainly requires mature and responsible individuals to deal with more and more choices; but in the end it may threaten the social contract itself and augur the return of the war of all against all. 'Anarchy yes, but not too much,' was one of the *graffiti* seen on a wall in Lisbon during the Portuguese revolution of 1975; it must have been written by a liberal. For it appears that now, rather than at the time at which Sartre and Marcel (to say nothing of Kierkegaard and Heidegger) first wrote, we have reached that nausea of disorientation which leads to pointless acts of identity-craving, terrorism perhaps, or to that more familiar reaction to anomie, suicide, and its numerous pre-figurations to which we have given acceptable names like stress, breakdown, and the like. The destruction of bonds has reduced human life chances to the point where the chances of survival are in jeopardy again.

What does this have to do with our question of the desirability of life chances and their link with liberty? I suggest a lot. We have quoted earlier Lionel Trilling's remark about liberalism and happiness. Trilling said this in a context which is relevant here. He spoke of the 'paradoxical relation' of liberalism to the emotions. On the one hand, liberals wanted people to be happy, but on the other hand they tended to deny emotions 'in their full possibility'. 'In the interests . . . of its vision of a general enlargement and freedom and rational direction of human life – [liberalism] drifts toward a denial of the emotions and the imagination.'[23] Would it be entirely unwarranted to trans-late this into the statement that the political theory of liberty has been so preoccupied with choice that it has failed to notice the importance of linkage?

I have left this argument to the end of this chapter and must therefore of necessity be more dogmatic than I like to be. The following reflection should thus be accompanied by a 'perhaps' throughout. Liberty is not a state of affairs, but a maxim of action. Societies may be more or less free, more or less pleasing to the liberal; but liberty remains under all circumstances a challenge and a task. It is the challenge which arises from the fundamental uncertainty of the human condition: since we do not know what is best for us, we must try to explore solutions. This requires in the first instance rules which prevent the dogmatization of error, that condition to which Popper has given the incomparable name, open society: 'But if we wish to remain human, there is only one way, the way into the open society. We must go into the unknown, the uncertain and insecure, using what reason we may have to plan for both security *and* freedom.'[24] As we now know, the juxtaposition is significant; it is yet another version of the function of options and ligatures.

Liberty is the absence of constraint, certainly. But this is merely the passive, negative side of the picture. All too often this negative side has dominated men's concerns, and has had to do so. Even so, the absence of constraint is not enough. The road into the unknown, the uncertain and insecure is also one towards the extension of human life chances. I am not saying that life chances are liberty. Liberty is a moral and political precept; life chances are a social concept. But the two are closely related in that the precept is about giving more people more opportunities in the sense of choices and linkages. Whether there will be progress or not, we do not know; but there might be progress. I despise that negative attitude which calls itself liberal, and is in fact little more than the defence of the vested interests of the haves; the *Constitution of Liberty* is only half a liberal book – it is profoundly lacking in imagination and courage. The active concept of liberty advocated here does not allow us to rest before all avenues of extending human life chances have been explored, and that means we must never rest. Liberalism is of necessity a philosophy of change.

This is not to say, of course, that the direction of change, or even the emphasis, is always the same. It is perfectly understandable that, for two centuries, liberals have concentrated on extending the horizon of choice at the risk of seeing linkages reduced and destroyed. But it makes equal sense to argue today – at any rate in the free societies of the OECD world – that the task of the liberal has to do with that most vexing of social objectives, building ligatures, encouraging the creation of norms, re-constituting the social contract. There are already several proposals before us. One may suspect that, in the end, solutions are more likely to be found around Nozick's 'minimal state' and Habermas's 'unconstrained communication' than in Rawls's 'justice', or any other social-democratic precept.[25] I also fear that the answers are not for governments to give, but that they have to grow; they can at best be encouraged, but are incapable of that deliberate action which characterized both

Keynesian economic policy and Beveridge's welfare state. This I fear not because I like government; on the contrary; but because it may mean that the contradictions of modernity swallow our potential of life chances before we have the opportunity to liberate it from the fetters of prevailing conditions. It is hard to contradict those who believe that the war of all against all will destroy us, either literally as in a nuclear holocaust, or metaphorically though equally effectively by the return first of private violence and then of crude public power.

Does this answer the question of why people should want the liberal quest for the extension of life chances? Happiness – to repeat the point – is undoubtedly desirable, but it is also an unlikely subject of social and political action. Welfare should probably be increased, though we must watch out that the concept does not turn into an instrument of the defence of privilege, or at any rate of the *status quo*, as gross national product has already done. Life chances provide us with opportunities, not just choices but meaningful choices, not just linkages but achievable linkages, and these opportunities make us grow. Not everybody wants to grow, to be sure; and at a time at which the theme of growth is more likely to be about linkages than about choices, it is quite likely that a conservative mood will spread. Not everybody has to be an active liberal; this is one of the fundamental tenets of the open society. But if we take the uncertainty of the human condition as given, and if we assume further that our life on earth has, or should have, meaning, then liberty as the quest for wider life chances for more people is not the worst objective.

3 Seven Notes on the Concept of Life Chances

I The Meaning and Significance of Concepts

Gottlob Frege has taught us that we must not ask for the meaning of words except in the context of sentences. It is *a fortiori* true for concepts (which do not have a 'natural' context) that they have meaning only in statements, and preferably in theoretical statements. In addition, Popper has reminded us of the nominalist article of faith that 'it is by no means clear what an empirical method for the definition of concepts would look like';[1] for while one can give a real object a name and call it The Anchorage, 'universal names' have no content. Thus there is no shortage of warnings against engaging in a purely conceptual discussion. We shall not ignore them; yet we intend to consider the concept from various aspects in these notes.

One of these aspects is almost biographical. To me, the concept of life chances in the form proposed here has become important on the occasion of two (related) practical concerns. One of these has to do with the comparison between German and British society. The impression is widespread that there are 'more life chances' in England than in Germany, and that this is so not merely with a view to the past, but even if one compares the 'rich' Federal Republic with the 'poor' Britain of today. There have been reports about German schoolchildren, who are always prone to moan about 'school stress' at home, praising extravagantly their experiences in British schools. Such widespread observations cannot be explained by the presence of more extended options in Britain; indeed these are undoubtedly more restricted. But it is characteristic of British society that for a number of reasons its ligatures have remained relatively undamaged where these have been broken several

times in Germany and may have gone to pieces in the end:
historical continuity oozes out of the pores of British society,
from the pomp of the guardsmen outside Buckingham Palace
to the almost endless chain of legal precedents in the courts; the
prevailing values of solidarity rather than individual competition (often misunderstood as a class structure) put a premium
on social bonds and linkages; throughout, individuals are
identified by where they belong rather than by what they have
achieved. It becomes apparent here that societies have the
weaknesses of their strengths, and vice versa; low valuation of
achievement promptly leads to low valuation of the currency;
but this is not the crucial point (nor are frequent revaluations a
sign of growing life chances). It is, rather, that the early, and
'organic' modernization of British society has permitted the
maintenance of a combination of linkages and choices for
which others envy the country (even though in the country
itself the options of others are regarded as a model by some).
The British example shows impressively that the desirable
objectives of the social process – what human societies are
about – are not simply alternatives or options. The German
example, on the other hand, shows that where modernization
is identified above all with options, with possibilities of choice,
something is missing.

What is it that is missing? It is important to beware of overly
romantic formulations; for that reason too I have chosen the
somewhat surgical expression 'ligatures' here. Nevertheless, it
must be said that stable bonds, or linkages, are one aspect of
life chances. Ligatures may of course be restrictions, indeed
fetters; conceivably, English society still has some way to go to
offer more people more options. But ligatures are values too;
their most important aspect is that they give meaning. History,
home, family, faith are typical elements of social linkages which
remove the individual from the vacuum of a merely 'optative'
society, bent on achievement and competition, and define his
or her place in the strict sense of the word.

This then is the other experience which has led me to the
complex concept of life chances: one may call it the de-coupling

of man in modern society, or the contradictions of modernity. The concept of options is dear to the liberal. To some extent, alternatives of choice are possibilities of freedom. If one cannot choose one's school, one's place of work, one's political party, one's holiday destination and many other things, one is not free. But the 'to some extent' is not to be underestimated. The mere opportunity of choice without a defined position from which to choose (in a sense without co-ordinates) is bound to remain random. The existentialist notion of an *acte gratuite* to which we have referred on several occasions, is after all not a joke; it means that every act, however horrible it may be, serves the one objective of proving one's identity. Mere opportunities for choice are the absence of morality; a world of mere options is beyond good and evil. This means, however, that the opportunities for choice lose their meaning; a feeling of pointlessness is spreading.

This is not the place to pursue the analysis of the contradictions of modernity (although there is no lack of hints in this volume). Otherwise we would have to look at the changing priorities of recent decades. For a long time, the extension of options was the dominant theme. But by now the abolition, or at any rate the reduction of ligatures which has accompanied the process – and it is a matter of theoretical importance that empirically this parallelism was no accident, though analytically it was not inevitable – has created its own set of problems. Anomie has become an element of the lives of many and notably of those who are still on the way to becoming full members of their societies; the teaching of history is reduced; the church becomes a christening and burying institution; mobility is a higher value than local loyalties; many families have cracked or frozen. In this way, an incomplete and empty modernity emerges which carries in it new and considerable dangers. We have put this in the phrase that the social contract itself becomes a problem again.

At this point, one line has to be drawn clearly. The argument advanced here is not a new version of the 'reversal of trends' ideology. Options do not become undesirable because the ligatures are missing which give them meaning. Nobody should misunderstand the implicit or explicit analyses of this volume as an invitation to return to the alleged homeliness of yesterday. This homeliness was a cage of bondage and not a house of liberty. The apparent relation of our analysis to some current discussions of the 'crisis of meaning' is misleading. But it is my view that a liberal position which aims at the extension of human life chances must have the formation of ligatures as much (and at times perhaps more) in mind as the opening-up of options.

The question of how one 'forms' ligatures, touches on one of the most difficult points of our understanding of society. This cannot be done by command – but that is just about the only answer which one can give with any degree of confidence. It is conceivable that there may be reliable patterns of 'unconstrained communication' which have the same social and individual effect as awareness of history, love of one's home, and religion. It may also be that new ligatures are already emerging which have so far escaped the eye of the social scientist (which does not begin to pass over reality before dusk is falling any more than that of the philosopher). So far, however, the more striking facts are the desperate and misguided forms of the search for bonds and ligatures, the mass suicide of the People's Temple sect, the mass suicide of heroin addicts, and the mass suicide of young people who are so disoriented that they misconstrue even the mildest demands on them as unbearable stress.

These are somewhat emotional, personal, and in any case pre-analytical remarks. They are meant to explain our interest in the concept of life chances, no more. But the claims which we have made for the concept go further. We have asserted that 'life chances' belong on that short list of basic concepts of social science which one would put together, were one to re-write the first chapter of Weber's *Economy and Society* today.[2] It is, in other words, a key concept, of which we have claimed that it plays a role in at least three intellectual contexts:

1 In the social theory of change and conflict the temptation is great to prefer formal statements for reasons of precision. I have done this myself with statements such as: Change is the more radical and rapid, the more intense and violent social conflicts are. Or: Social conflicts arise from structures of authority and are about these structures. However, such statements remain unsatisfactory, because they are lacking substantive definition. The question is whether there are substantive definitions which do not transcend the requirements of theory altogether and lead into randomness. If there are such definitions, their analytical strength would be considerable. It may be that the concept of life chances achieves this objective.

2 Inevitably, the social theory of change – at any rate, if it includes substantive elements – touches and crosses the boundary to the attempt to make sense of history. (I prefer this expression to the heavier one of a 'meaning of history'; what we are concerned with is the attempt to make the historical process plausible, in the terms which we have discussed in the first chapter of this volume.) As we have seen, this is both a scientific problem and an inescapable question. The concept of life chances can help to provide such plausibility of history.

3 Even if one regards it as possible to draw the line between theoretical analysis and normative design clearly, the task of designing desirable patterns remains important, indeed imperative; here too, silence is itself an answer. As a rule, and for good reason, political theory steers clear of ultimate objectives. It makes sense in particular not to blur the line between legitimate objectives of social and political action on the one hand, and the individual's search for a definitive meaning of life on the other; merging politics and religion has rarely done societies any good. But in order to define the legitimate objectives of social and political action clearly, we need once again a substantive category, and the concept of life chances may help us in this respect.

Is it not asking too much of a concept to give it three functions in this way? In the end, the proof of the pudding will have to be in the eating. But one might argue that a concept which aims at the substantive dimension of social change forms almost as a matter of course a hinge between social-science theory, philosophy of history, and political theory (some would say theory of society).

Instead of a systematic attempt to map this conceptual field, we shall try to find out about it here in several distinct and different approaches. First, we shall yet again describe, perhaps define, the place of the concept (II). Then I want to supplement, in a kind of self-correction, earlier approaches to the theory of conflict and change by introducing the concept of life chances into them (III). The exegesis of Weber's concept of chance comes closest to 'pure' conceptual analysis (IV). Time and again we have spoken of measuring life chances, and of operationalizing the concept; if we describe attempts to do so as games, this should not be misread to mean that they are pointless (V). The somewhat loose introductory remarks to this chapter have made the proximity of our deliberations to Robert Merton's analysis of social structure and anomie apparent; we shall pursue the subject further (VI). Finally, a few loose ends concerning problems of political theory arising from the relationship of life chances and liberty have to be joined (VII).

II Further on the Theoretical Place of the Concept of Life Chances

The concept of life chances has a context of meaning in terms of each of the three methodological aspects: social-science theory, philosophy of history, and political theory. Here we shall try yet again, starting from philosphy of history, to determine the place of the concept in social science and consider some of its implications.

What is human society and its history about? It is, says one, about the unfolding of a divine plan right across the wishes and fears of men towards the end of salvation. The hidden power of the world spirit, says another, takes human society through many a thesis and antithesis eventually to the realization of the moral ideal in the supreme order of the state. The third says that if there is an intention in the history of human communities at all, it would follow from the nature of man as a reasonable being that this must consist of the eternal peace of a society of world citizens. History, says the fourth, is the birth of man in the fullness of his capacities by his own social activity. None of these approaches is entirely in line with the attempt which we have made in the introductory chapter to this volume, not even the fourth one which by its organic analogy ('birth', 'fullness of his capacities') evokes the suspicion of a fundamentally closed image of history. History is the progressive development of man by his own activity; but it is a continuing, possibly forever incomplete process of (possible) growth. This is the only way in which we can give an active rather than a resigned answer to Kant's bitter question of what is the meaning and the place of earlier generations, and with what right we declare our ancestors mere instruments for our own higher objectives[3]: as a moral challenge, liberty remains the same throughout history; no generation is 'better' than earlier ones. But the attainment of this objective means that human beings can continue to grow, to be more (or indeed less) human, which in turn means that we not only need an open society in order to permit freedom, but that history is open.

However, this is not the thread of analysis which I want to pursue at this point. It may be pleasing, and even exciting to advance an idea of the origin and objective of history. But the response to the questions of what human society and its history are about, which we are seeking here, is not meant to be pleasing or even exciting; it is meant to be useful: for describing society, for analyzing its laws of development, thus for social theory, and in the end even for laying the foundations of political theory. Thus we are not concerned with metaphysics camouflaged as philosophy of history, but with a fundamental problem of social science.

Societies are fields of social roles. Man finds himself, at least in his incarnation as *homo sociologicus*, that is in the laser beam of scientific analysis, confronted with a plurality of expectations which he may not have invented but which he cannot escape either. Such expectations are crystallized around social positions: man, father, teacher, member of the Middletown Football Club. They are not random or arbitrary; for they are protected by sanctions; whoever transgresses rules is called to order, and this is why most do not transgress rules. In this way, the abstract and distant entity 'society' becomes quite real for people, as neighbours, colleagues, as offices and courts, as promotions and tax rebates, as hopes and fears. Roles, that is expectations crystallized around positions, are themselves a part of wider fields: families, communities, enterprises, associations, regions, countries. Thus, wherever we look, society is structure, rules, and the guarding of rules, and people are agents of social structure even where they break rules. But what is it that is structured in this way? It is not people of course; but what are roles, expectations, sanctions related to? What is, as it were, the substratum of social structure, that to which all expectations of power and influence, property and income, fame and prestige are related? What, in other words, fills the shaky skeleton, the structure of roles and positions in their interrelations, with flesh and with colour?

Societies are process too; they do not stand still. Whoever describes them as static misses the motive forces of the field and creates a suspiciously mild image of utopia. The expectations crystallized in social roles are not merely reflections of the norms which are binding on all members of a society, but they are also expectations of allegiance to particular groups, thus interests. Interests not only differ, they are controversial; the struggle of interest groups and their latent basis in social categories is an unmistakable part of social reality. Moreover, this struggle is a productive force; it brings about change, in that hitherto neglected interests succeed, piecemeal, more radically, and occasionally in a fundamental process of transformation called revolution. The theory of social change begins with such phenomena, although they are no more than a beginning. Like the question of the substratum of social structures, that of the motives of social change is crucial: What is it that introduces unrest into human societies? What are controversial interests and their social formations about? What is therefore the direction of the processes which move human societies? Where is the driving force of history?

There is a theoretically important, though still formal, answer to this question, and an equally important, apparently objective, indeed world-spiritual counterweight to it. The formal answer is in the phenomenon of power, the key phenomenon of social structures and processes. Social roles are structured in fields in accordance with the signals given from positions of power or authority. Like currencies, structures of income and prestige have their own laws to some extent; but in the last analysis they are derived from other structures. Social stratification rests on power, and so does the entire system of social norms and of the sanctions accompanying them. Moreover, relations of power or authority are not merely the distributive centre of the structure of the social field; they are also the starting point and focus of conflicts which generate change. In their formal aspect, social conflicts are always about the retention or acquisition of power; interest groups are formed around this objective; and it is no accident that those who express their interests pay attention above all to governmental structures. In this formal sense, power is the key category for the analysis of both social structures and social processes. Without power there is no society.

If one wants to look at society primarily from the point of view of their laws of development, thus of change, one will inevitably wish to tie power relations to other more 'objective' conditions. Marx has done this convincingly, though with (pardonable) over-specificity. He argued that in its visible aspect change is always change of relations of production, of prevailing norms. But there is a less visible aspect of change; it consists of forces of production, which by contrast to relations of production are not intrinsically conservative, but grow steadily. At certain points of development, however, this development is held up by the rigidity of prevailing conditions;

feudal structures of ownership leave no room for the require-ments of industrial production. This is the time at which suppressed classes have the opportunity to reverse relations of power in the name of newly awakened forces of production. This kind of presentation generalizes Marx's thesis in important respects. (In the following note, we shall be somewhat more specific.) The issue is not merely 'production', its patterns and its potential. The point is, rather, that social conflicts lead to orgasms whenever a demanding class has the real socio-economic potential of the time on its side. Power gets weaker, the more it tries to defend antiquated structures. More gener-ally, structures of authority are themselves tied to a socio-economic field which determines their chances and limits.

All this, however, still leaves open the question with which we started this note: what is human society and its history about? Power is certainly important – but can one simply assume that it is desirable as such, a value in itself? Certainly not. There are not only people who, for whatever reason, do not desire power (Nietzsche may despise them, the unworldly asceticist may praise them), but even those who seek power do so as a rule, or at any rate frequently, as an instrument for doing something. It is not power as such, but what one can do with it that seems desirable. What are, after all, forces of produc-tion and relations of production? Relations organize something – but what? And forces are a new potential – but for what? Time and again, the formal analysis reaches its limits and thus raises the question of the substratum of social structures, the motive of social processes.

Thomas Hobbes has given one answer to this question, and one that differs from that of other authors who were concerned with the purpose of history. Hobbes's answer is simply that the structure and process of society are about survival. Since every man is by nature the other's wolf, and thus the state of nature a war of all against all, and since in view of this disposition nobody could be sure in this state to see the sun rise tomorrow, people agree on those minimum rules and institutions which guarantee their survival. (Rousseau with his romantic love of nature saw the social contract differently, and the French Revolution in implementing Rousseau has consequently paid less attention to survival, but we shall follow the more realistic Englishman, Hobbes.) Thus the police, the courts, the rules that apply to them and the governments that make and supervise them have their foundation. The minimal state which emerges from this kind of argument has recently been described again by Robert Nozick who concludes somewhat haltingly and hesitantly that in the end there is no justification for public power except to safeguard survival.[4]

I shall not argue this case, but the question remains whether it describes what happens. Admittedly, state and society increase the survival chances of men; clearly the minimal state is determined, both in terms of its substratum and its motives, by human survival chances; but the communities in which we are living are equally clearly not sufficiently described in this manner. More than that, there is no human community in memory, history or anthropology which has confined itself to safeguarding the survival chances of its citizens. Whatever doubts one may raise in the legitimacy of the welfare society, however evident it may be that its reality leaves something to be desired, it is certainly not minimal – and our question of the purposes of human society is a question about real societies.

If the minimal answer does not suffice, and the philosophy of survival does not help us, we need other yardsticks of human desire. For this much is clear: the substratum and motive of society are intentions, interests, needs, instincts, wishes, expectations and hopes – there is apparently no shortage of words – of the people who have concluded the social contract, or at any rate accepted it without protest. But the attempt to understand them takes us back to the subjects which we have criticized as we introduced the concept of life chances: happiness, utility, welfare. In more popular understanding, they usually appear in one of two shapes: as the philosophy of money, and as the philosophy of happiness.

All human needs and wants, says Milton Friedman, can be expressed in money terms.[5] A bottle of wine? Two dollars, or maybe twenty. A journey to the South? Two hundred dollars. A car? Two thousand dollars. A house? Twenty thousand dollars. A little time? A little power? A little freedom? There is nothing (or so some argue) that could not be expressed in dollars and cents, not even life itself. How much is your life worth? The question is rarely put in monetary terms, and yet it can be answered as such. In any case, official statistics measure the possibility of meeting human needs in this way: *per capita* income, expressed as national income divided by 'heads' of the population. Under one thousand dollars? A developing country. Above ten thousand dollars? A rich country. There is by now a considerable literature on social indicators other than income, and we shall return to it; but on the whole the spirit of the times is with Friedman: in capitalist countries, though by no means only in them, the money one has (and often, paradoxically, especially in communist countries, the dollars one had) is regarded as a measure of one's ability to satisfy needs and wants.

It is not surpising that this financial cynicism has found enemies. One of the most extreme among them is Sicco Mansholt. Under the impression of the first report of the Club of Rome and the beginnings of the environmental movement, and further supported by the emotional experience of the oil crisis in the winter of 1973, he has fought the old standards in his characteristic manner: what matters is not gross national product, but 'gross human happiness', and this is attained more easily where there is no abundance of dollars[6]. Mankind must change its standards in order to find what really counts, a satisfaction which money cannot provide, a feeling of satisfaction based on truly important values.

It was obviously easy for the monetarists to take Mansholt to pieces. Even apart from the *argumentum ad hominem* that the advocate was not exactly speaking from a rostrum of poverty, it is evident that most of the things which Mansholt had in mind cost money and can thus be had for money: clean air, pure water, better transport, better forests and parks, more pleasant houses, more leisure time, and the like. Money is in the last analysis merely an instrument for satisfying those wishes which lead to happiness, and happiness is in the last analysis merely the subjective sensation which accompanies the satisfaction of such wishes. Both, incidentally, need a flourishing, if not an explosively expanding economy, in order to allow people to satisfy their wishes.

We do not have to choose between the two philosophies. Both are right in dealing with human wishes and sources of their satisfaction. The truth is somewhere outside their coordinates: we can most certainly not buy everything, neither love nor creative forces nor sports talent, not even health, nor time within fairly narrow limits, not faith and not hope, and not freedom either. And other things which one can buy, such as systems of public transport, or sewerage, or housing are human rights even for those who cannot pay for them; thus they may be, but should not be, up for sale. The currency of money is too alien, too much subject to its own rules, moreover too much in the hands of those who administer it, use it, increase or restrict its quantity. Happiness on the other hand is too little of a currency, too much a matter of personal sentiment, too arbitrary, neither measurable nor tradeable, a feeling which escapes the grip of society to a considerable extent, even if society influences its conditions.

This then describes the horizon in which we seek an answer: an answer to the question of what human society is about; the substratum of social structure; the motive of social processes; the substance even of relations of power and of the dialectics of relations and forces of production; more than survival chances in the reality of human societies; somewhere between the philosophy of money and the philosophy of happiness, that is the assumption that everything can be measured in dollar terms, and the other assumption that the individual alone knows what has value – in short, a category which expresses human wants and needs, interests and hopes in a way that does not suppress the subjective element but makes it clear that one is seeking more than the personal sensation of happiness, namely, socially structured ways of individual life.

The category which serves these multiple purposes is that of life chances. Human societies and their history are about life chances, not about the greatest happiness of the greatest number, but about the greatest life chances of the greatest number. Life chances are (in principle) measurable possibilities to realize needs, wants and interests in, or at times against, a given social context. They are the substratum of social structures, in which life chances are therefore organized. They are also the motive force of social processes, which are therefore about life chances.

III Life Chances, Class Conflict, Social Change: a Self-Correction

The subject of my earlier work on social theory remains my primary concern: how do open societies remain open, and how do others become that way? In one respect, answering this question is a minimal programme of freedom. We are living in a world of uncertainty in which our answers may be, and often are, wrong; if we want to avoid the tyranny of error, we must avoid all tyranny and make sure that it remains possible to give new answers, and to give them effectively. The capacity of societies to change is a necessary – although not a sufficient – condition of liberty. There are philosophical questions arising from this theme, relating to the ethics of uncertainty in general, and the moral tenets of an experimental anthropology as it is implied by such a view. There are questions of political theory. Is what we have come to call democracy – or representative government, or the separation of powers, or the rule of law – the appropriate method for institutionalizing openness? There are practical questions in this context. What does one do to prevent German society from falling back into dangerous stagnation, as appeared to threaten it at the time of the Grand Coalition of 1966–9? How can one contribute to opening up those societies which are still existing under various tyrannies? Then there are theoretical questions in the stricter sense, questions of scientific theories. What forces determine the rate, the range and the direction of social change? How can we explain the processes which make for change, and which are set free by open institution? In this note, as in much of my earlier work, I shall concentrate on the latter, theoretical aspect; but I want to add that while I have always respected the need to distinguish between the various dimensions of action and analysis, I have never believed in keeping them apart at all cost. The social scientist must do more than merely pursue social science.[7] Concern with the theory of social processes is barren if it is based on no more than a detached theoretical interest.

In this respect, I have little disagreement with the greatest theorist of social change, Karl Marx. In other respects, his brilliant fallacies are a starting line rather than a finishing post of analysis. In his theory of change, Marx superimposed two historical experiences which had little if anything to do with each other at the time, although they came to be linked in practice as well as in theory in our own century. One is the French Revolution of 1789, and more precisely the previously unheard-of fact that large numbers of people – 'the crowd' – could play a major part in historical change ('whether [in the words of George Rudé] the revolutionary crowd is represented as "*la canaille*" or "vile multitude" by Taine and Burke; as "Victorious Anarchy" by Carlyle; or as "*le peuple*" or "*tout Paris*" by Michelet and Aulard'[8]). A theory of (revolutionary) change by class conflict evoked almost necessarily the picture of more or less organized masses clashing with the forces of law and order and finally storming the Bastille. The other experience which went into Marx's theory is that of the Industrial Revolution, and more precisely of technical inventions increasing the productive potential of an economy enormously, although their adoption requires painful changes in almost all aspects of social relations. From the reception given to Stephenson's 'Rocket' to the desperate rearguard action of the Luddites there are many examples of such growing pains. In a sense, the French Revolution was about citizenship, and the Industrial Revolution about prosperity, and one of the fallacies of their *ex post* combination was the belief that the two necessarily go together.

But Marx's theory is neither all fallacy nor is it above all unimpressive. Classes, according to Marx, are groups intertwined in a relation of fatal conflict by virtue of the places which their members occupy in the political economy. Inevitably, one class defends the *status quo* of legal norms, political power and economic distribution, even though some of its enlightened members may desert the cause and become sociologists. Equally inevitably, the other class demands its own place in the sun, a fundamental change in social, political and economic relations. Neither class, however, advances its case out of the blue, as it were. Rather, the analysis of class conflict is linked to that of what Marxians like to call, somewhat misleadingly, 'objective' processes, that is developments of social structure which are not as such the product of class action. Ruling classes inherit certain structures, 'relations of production'. It is these which they defend, a system of ownership, a method of wage payment, a type of responsibility for others, feudal bonds rather than contracts, for example. Existing structures provide the substance of their interests. This is relatively easy to see; here as elsewhere the other aspect of the link between the two revolutions is more important. For Marx assumes that oppressed classes do not simply act out of resentment against their oppression, for negative or protest reasons. In any case, their actions are not likely to be effective, insofar as they are merely a reaction born out of frustration. They act, rather, in the name of a new potential for satisfying wants and needs, of new 'forces of production'. It is the steam engine which gave the early bourgeoisie its pathos and its clout, not its resentment of feudal privilege; and the weakness of feudal relations was not that they were unjust, but that they prevented the establishment of an industrial mode of production which is among other things based on contractual relations of work (or so Marx believed on the strength of the English example).

This is an impressive approach: organized socio-political groups, growing out of a wider potential of support under

C

specified conditions, are engaged in a struggle for power as the visible exponents of the present and the future, the former embodied in the laws and institutions of a society, and the latter represented by the potential of production and thus presumably of bringing well-being to people. There is a sense in which this describes what happened in Russia in 1917 ('electricity' was after all one of Lenin's promises), and perhaps what has happened in many other countries since. It describes much less well what happened in Britain, in France, or in any of the other countries which we today call developed. We cannot pursue the reasons and implications of this consequential misunderstanding here. But I would suggest that one reason is that Marx's approach was terminologically, if not substantively, dated. He was so fascinated by the new potential of industrial *production* and by the way in which it was first repressed and then released by prevailing structures of social relations, that he overlooked the much more general figure of development of which the Industrial Revolution is merely a special case. This is Aristotle's dialectic of δύναμις and ἐνέργεια, of potential and actuality, of that which could be and that which is. The potential which is suppressed by prevailing social structures may be one of production, but it may also be one of distribution, or indeed one of organization, for example the organization of work, leisure, education and retirement, and thus the social construction of human lives. One is in fact concerned with the much more general phenomenon of an emerging and maturing potential of life chances being held back – or not, as the case may be – by a prevailing reality of social organization.

This is a relatively simple amendment of Marx's theory. It is also a consequential amendment of my own fragmentary theories as proposed in my book on *Class and Class Conflict.*[9] There, I concentrated very largely on the French Revolution part of Marx's theory, that is on the theory of class organization and of what one might call the mechanics of class conflict. Critics have rightly complained about the curiously formalistic character of such an approach, in which the question of what class conflict is about is answered by little else than the reference to the '*status quo*', its defence or the attack on it. I have said of course that the substance of class interests arises from social positions and is in that sense structural, or even 'objective', but the central proposition in this context sounds more like a definition than like a theoretical statement:

Our model of conflict group analysis involves the proposition that of the two aggregates of authority positions to be distinguished in every association, one – that of domination – is characterized by an interest in the maintenance of a social structure that for them conveys authority, whereas the other – that of subjection – involves an interest in changing a social condition that deprives its incumbents of authority.[10]

It is in keeping with this approach that the dimensions of conflict discussed in the theory are those of intensity and of violence, and the dimensions of change those of radicalness and rapidity. I see no reason today for denying the usefulness of such an analysis, but it is also limited, for what is left out is the most important if the most complex dimension: that of the direction of change and of the substance of conflict. One way of introducing this dimension is by borrowing Marx's (or Aristotle's) approach in the sense of linking the analysis of class to the analysis of non-class developments of social structure which have to do with potential and actuality, with what a society could offer and what it actually offers. These social offerings in turn have to be expressed in structural terms other than, or at least more general than, 'production'. I propose to follow this path, and I suggest that it marks one of the points at which the concept of life chances becomes crucial for the analysis of social processes.

So far as Marx is concerned, I have presented a rather truncated version of his theory of change so far. That was deliberate, for I find the remaining elements much less relevant, and much more fallacious too. However, it may be worth looking at them briefly, if only in order to define one aspect of the problems discussed time and again in this volume which has not yet been mentioned here, that of progress.

There is first of all the fact that Marx, rather than explain the direction of change, in fact makes assumptions about it. Take the concept of mode or relations of production. Marx finds it either difficult or impracticable to conceive of social structure – of relations of production – as changing in an undramatic and continuing fashion. He assumes that relations of production are in fact unchanging or virtually unchanging. At any rate this is so for the duration of a stage or epoch of history. Prevailing norms relating to property, to work and its conditions, to systems of production, distribution and consumption, but also to the various layers of superstructure, are in a strange sense 'ready', both in the sense of being fully prepared and in that of being complete, when they become valid; they come about by a kind of revolutionary big bang, and the only change of which they are capable afterwards is a radical change which makes them disappear as such, the creation of what Marx sometimes calls a new 'basis', a new 'stage of historical development'. All change of social structures is revolutionary change.

I have discussed the shortcomings of this approach elsewhere.[11] Suffice it to say here that the stop-go image of social structure neither corresponds to observed facts nor does it lend itself to satisfactory explanations. The fact is that societies change all the time; and if we wait for revolutions as the only permissible form of change, we are likely to have to construct absurd theoretical crutches such as the numerous attempts on the part of more or less sophisticated Marxians to prove that everything, but everything that has happened since the turn of the century, the Great Depression and fascism, the Second World War and the Cold War, the energy crisis and the North-South dialogue, inflation and unemployment is but a symptom of the crisis of capitalism. So what? Without pursuing the theme any further here, I would suggest that it is much more useful to work on an assumption which modifies Newton's first law of movement and states that societies are in a state of continuing, uniform and linear development unless certain factors intervene to decelerate or accelerate, confirm or deflect the process.

Again, the critical aspect of Marx's assumptions concerns not the relations, but the forces of production. While relations of production remain unchanged throughout an epoch, productive forces change all the time. In fact, Marx uses the term almost invariably in the context of 'developments', or 'stages of development' of productive forces. It is plausible to interpret his many references to this effect to mean that Marx thinks of productive forces as continuously growing throughout history; indeed history is designed to make them grow all the time. Relations of production are a response to a certain stage of development of productive forces; but these forces expand and grow. They outgrow the structure of an epoch, and as the resulting contradictions increase, the epoch begins to wilt and decay, or, less metaphorically (though Marx himself uses the organic metaphor), a revolutionary situation begins to develop. Marx is not naive enough to assume a unilinear, monorhythmic growth of forces of production; in bourgeois society, for example, the process is greatly accelerated; but he assumes throughout that the potential of societies to satisfy wants grows and grows.

This presentation of Marx's approach may be incomplete, but it is not misleading. It is true that Marx had in mind technological developments among other things, and it is generally assumed that science and technology at least have tended to grow in volume, effectiveness and by any other index. Elsewhere, Marx plays with the word wealth, or rather, *Reichtum*, richness, in relation to forces of production. He speaks of 'the degree of development of the material forces of production and thus of richness'; and most people would probably subscribe to the proposition that poverty has on the whole decreased in history (although Arnold Toynbee was not the only author to voice doubts about the effects of the Industrial Revolution in this respect).[12] In any case, Marx then refers to 'the highest development of productive forces ... and thus the richest development of individuals', and clearly does not mean that individuals are, or are going to be, very wealthy. On the contrary, this sounds more like that 'universality of the individual not as a figment of imagination, but as universality of his real and ideal relations' which he regards as characteristic of a society in which 'the full development of productive forces has become a condition of production'. I do not think that one is misrepresenting Marx if one imputes to him the assumption that the potential of human development has grown throughout history.[13]

This assumption, however, is probably implausible. It is at the very least subject to grave doubts. What about those less optimistic minds who regard human history since the seventeenth century as a story of continuous decline? Nearer general understanding perhaps, what about the thesis that from a certain point onwards the generalization of opportunities leads to a reduction of their worth? (Are productive forces always options, or could they be ligatures as well?) In any case, what about centuries of stagnation and, worse, of regression in many measurable respects? Progress is too precarious a notion for us to assume that it is automatic, or even general in any respect; if there is such a thing as progress with respect to human life chances and the development of human nature corresponding to them, a case would have to be made rather than assumed. It appears that Marx, like all his colleagues in the new field of political economy, was somewhat over-impressed by the experience of economic expansion around him.

In the case of Marx, the readiness to be so impressed was helped by his philosophical predilections. He could never rid himself of the Hegelian sickness of having to try to make sense of the process of history by assuming unsatisfactory beginnings and a totally satisfactory end. The quotation about the 'full development of productive forces' is but one of many which show that throughout Marx assumed not only progress within historical phases – at least progress of productive forces and revolutionary energies – but also a progression of such phases right up to the imminent final revolution and the perfect society which is to follow it. Karl Popper has said all there is to be said about this approach.[14] Insofar as we are concerned here with the course and the meaning of history, no attempt will be made to describe the process in its entirety, let alone to assert or project perfection. Our approach to understanding the historical process, and progress, is not Hegel's, but Kant's:

History, which is concerned with the story [of human actions], however deeply their causes may be hidden, nevertheless lets us hope: that if it regards the play of man's freedom of will *in toto,* it may discover that it follows a regular course; and that in this manner, what strikes the eye in individual subjects as confused and irregular, may nevertheless be capable of being recognized in the entire species as a steadily progressing, though slow unfolding of its original endowments.[15]

I began this section by restating my own concern with change and identifying the lacunae which I found in earlier approaches to the understanding of social processes. The most obvious gap is that in *Class and Class Conflict,* where the analysis of conflict remains highly formal and little is said about either the substance of conflict or the direction of change. The same is true for most of my other writings on the theory of conflict. By introducing the notion of life chances as the subject matter of human social development, it may be possible to go some way towards remedying this deficiency. Social conflicts are about more life chances, or about the defence of the level which they have reached, respectively, that is to say (from the point of view of those in power) about the attempt to secure the options which have turned into privileges within the framework of prevailing linkages or ligatures, and (from the point of view of those excluded from power) about the realization of new options even at the expense of familiar ligatures, or at times about the creation of a new quality of ligatures. In this way, a bridge to the understanding of progress can be built. If one succeeded in rendering the concept of life chances sufficiently operational to make statements possible about whether there are in a given society, or for a given class, more or fewer life chances, then the problem of progress could be reformulated in a way which is equally interesting in empirical and in theoretical contexts.

There is one other point which deserves mention in this connection. Life chances are opportunities for individual development provided by social structure, 'moulds', as we have called them. As such, they provide an important bridge between an understanding of society which emphasizes the structural quality of things social – *faits sociaux* in the strict sense of Durkheim – and a normative theory of society which emphasizes individual liberty. I do not think that I have succeeded in my *Homo Sociologicus* in providing a satisfactory solution of the problem which I have posed in that essay. The juvenile anarchism of the dream of a freedom which is essentially freedom *from* society leads to consequences and actions which solve little if anything. But a solution is necessary, at any rate if one is concerned, as I am, with the conditions of liberty *in* society. Again, I would certainly not claim that such a solution can be found in a concept. But the concept of life chances may help formulate statements which lead some way towards the better understanding of liberty in society. We have begun to try this path, and we shall continue along it.

IV Max Weber's Concept of 'Chance'

Max Weber liked the concept of 'chance', because he knew that there is freedom, and this not only in statistical theory, but as an 'uncertainty relation' in the real world, thus of the possibility that things do not happen which we would 'normally' expect to happen. But Weber also liked the concept of 'chance' because he believed that human societies are above all about opening spaces, for 'chances of acquisition', 'exchange chances', 'supply chances', 'chances of domination', 'preferential chances', 'future chances', for life chances. And somewhere between probability theory and sociology the useful word 'chance' becomes indispensable for him; it becomes a category. If one considers the more than one hundred places in the first volume of *Economy and Society* alone, at which Weber uses chance as a word or a category, one cannot but be surprised about how little attention the literature on Weber has paid to the term, and even more, how naively and without reflection Weber himself has tended to use a concept which provides a key both to his method and to the substance of his thought.

These statements require some reservations on closer inspection. The following interpretation will make it abundantly clear that Weber's use of the term was not entirely 'naive'. And so far as the literature on Weber is concerned, there are a number of discussions of the concept of 'chance', for example, in the books by Schumann, Siberski, and above all Hufnagel.[16] Hufnagel's thoughtful interpretation, however, shows how limited the understanding of the concept has remained so far. Time and again he speaks of Weber's 'operational category of "chance", determined as it is by methodological nominalism and the cautiousness of the positivistic empiricist'.[17] We shall find that this is at best one aspect of Weber's concept. In doing so, and for the purposes of the present exegesis, we shall confine ourselves almost entirely to the first volume of *Economy and Society*, in which the term appears frequently and which permits a full analysis of its meaning. (We shall also use our own translation of Max Weber's text: for in most English translations the 'German' word *Chance* has been rendered in interpretive rather than literal ways, more often than not as 'probability'.)

The very first use of the concept in *Economy and Society* demonstrates the manner in which Max Weber combines method and substance:

The 'laws', as one has come to call some doctrines of a sociology of understanding – such as Gresham's law, for example – are observation-confirmed typical *chances* of a process of social action which is to be expected if certain conditions are given and which becomes understandable in terms of typical motives and typically intended meaning on the part of the actors.[18]

If one allows oneself not to be put off by it, this is a fascinating manner of words. One can see Weber's pen hesitating as he is describing social laws. In the end he cannot bring himself to say that such laws describe social processes as they typically happen, but he has to add a reservation: they describe the chance that such processes happen. Laws are not unreservedly true; in establishing them, one has to take into account the possibility that what they stipulate will in fact not occur. This reservation, or caution, can be found throughout Weber's work. 'The constitution of an association shall mean the factual chance of obedience to the authority which is imposing its will.[19] Many others would have left the words 'chance of' out and simply spoken of factual obedience as the characteristic of the constitution. ' "Law" for us is an "order" with certain specific guarantees for . . .', and now he does not say 'the empirical validity of norms' (although this would have been perfectly all right, because legal sanctions are about making sure that rules hold in practice), but instead he says: 'for the chance of their empirical validity'; the kind of order which we call law contains elements which make it – what? possible? probable? plausible? – that the rules which it embodies will actually hold.

The question in parenthesis has considerable significance, for the apparent epistemological reservation contained in Weber's use of the term 'chance' is more than that. Weber may wish to phrase things in a cautious or modest way, but there is more to it. Wherever he says 'chance', word and concept have a definite meaning. This is clearly not the meaning of the English word 'chance'.[20] One is not talking about things being a matter of pure chance, or about chance in roulette, that is about random probability or mere possibility. (John Stuart Mill at one point talks about the imperfections of the world and the need to forego happiness in order to be truly happy, and adds: 'For nothing except that consciousness can raise a person above the chances of life, by making him feel that, let fate and fortune do their worst, they have no power to subdue him.'[21] But however nice it is to find 'chances of life', in an English author, he does mean the vicissitudes, contingencies, the imponderables which happen apparently at random.) Surprising as this may seem, it could be argued that Weber uses the concept of chance in almost the opposite sense of its English meaning; it signifies anything but mere possibility. There is a point where he defines the difference between legal and sociological ways of looking at things. Having defined legal analysis by the 'normative meaning' which 'should pertain to a legal norm in a logically correct manner', he has this to say about sociological analysis:

The latter on the other hand asks what in fact happens in a community, because there is the chance that people who participate in

community action, among them in particular those in whose hands
rests a socially relevant measure of factual influence on this community action, regard certain orders as subjectively valid and treat
them as such, so that their own action is oriented to them.[22]

The importance of this statement is that it clarifies the relation
between factual action and chances. At first sight, one might
think that, for Weber, 'chance' is a probabilistic term: the
'chance of obedience' as the probability of obedience, the
'chance of validity' as the probability of validity. Here and
there, Weber in fact makes statements which seem to confirm
this impression: 'An order shall be called . . . law, if it is exter-
nally guaranteed by the chance of physical or mental force. . . .'[23]
A legal order (one might say by way of interpretation) rests on
the probability, calculable in principle, that those who transgress its rules will be hit by sanctions. In fact, Weber says at one
point, turning the statement round, as it were, that 'calculable
chances' arise for the individual from the validity of legal
norms.[24] But at precisely this point it becomes clear that Weber
is not simply thinking of statements about the factual probability of a certain course of events when he uses 'chance', for
the statement about the law being guaranteed by the chance of
force continues like this: '. . . by the action of a staff of people
specially instituted for the purpose of enforcing conformity or
punishing violations'. For Weber the probability of sequences
of action postulated in the concept of chance is not merely an
observed and thus calculable probability, but it is a probability
which is invariably anchored in given structural conditions.
Thus, chance means probability on the grounds of causal relations, or structurally determined probability.

We merely note in passing here that this kind of approach
implies a certain notion of sociology; contrary to life chances,
this notion of Weber's has often been discussed, usually in connection with the term *Verstehen*.[25] Sociology is about an understanding of structures ('certain facts and events') which make a
determinate behaviour regularly probable. The epistemological
reservation of the concept of chance imposes limitations on any
simple causal connection of given structures and observed

behaviour, and this not merely because of the imperfections of our knowledge, but also because the relationship between norm and action, structure and behaviour is of necessity tenuous.

Another aspect of this concept of chance is more important for our analysis. Weber builds into the probability aspect of his concept of chance a reference to real, thus externalized, not to say alienated structures (of society); this enables him to use the term among other things (though not exclusively) for the probability that a given behaviour is effective by reason of objective conditions, in that sense for objectively given probabilities of behaviour. This is a complicated idea which is best explained by an example. In his 'Basic Concepts', Weber distinguishes between open and closed social relations:

A social relationship [defined earlier as a chance that people act socially in a manner capable of meaningful explanation] can offer its participants chances of satisfying internal or external interests, whether in terms of their purpose or their success, whether by solidary action or by conciliation. If participants expect from their advocacy an improvement of their own chances in terms of extent, kind, security, or value, they are interested in its openness, if on the other hand they expect something from monopolization, they are interested in closing it to the outside.

A closed social relationship may guarantee its participants monopolized chances (a) freely, or (b) regulated or rationed in extent and kind, or (c) appropriated to individuals permanently and absolutely or even irremovably (closure to the inside). Appropriated chances shall be called 'rights'.[26]

It is not easy to disentangle this thoughtful statement, although it is probably necessary to do so, if one does not want to lose the subtlety of the argument.

It is not the intention of this exegesis to impute to Weber an unambiguous concept of chance throughout; by avoiding terminological definition, he has kept several possibilities open. A certain hiatus is therefore unmistakable as between chance as a structurally anchored probability of behaviour on the one hand (as in his definition of social relationship), and chance as something which the individual can actually have, such as the chance of satisfying interests. In the latter case, the behavioural aspect has become crystallized, objectivated. Thus, 'improvement of one's chances' becomes the enhancement of the probability that one's own behaviour will have certain results in that others respond in a certain manner. This objective concept of chance has one feature in common with the one describing behaviour, and that is that in both cases probability is anchored in structure. Chances of satisfying interests exist because there are (for example, open or closed) social relationships, they are not simply suspended in mid-air. Chances themselves are socially determined. Social structures are arrangements of chances.

Let us remember then that chance for Weber always means structurally anchored probabilities of the occurrence of certain events. These events may be actual human behaviour, such as the observation of legal norms, they may also be crystallized human behaviour, such as predictable action, including above all the satisfaction of interests. The remainder of this exegesis will be concerned with this second aspect of chances, that is with their crystallized or objective incarnation.

Weber uses the objective concept of chance freely and extensively in the context of the analysis of economic issues:

A kind of economic dependence which occurs very frequently in all forms of human community is brought about by competition for economic chances: offices, clientele, opportunity for profit from occupation or work, or the like.[27]

Thus, economic chances are probabilities of satisfying interests and needs which accrue from the position which a person holds in the process of production and distribution of scarce goods. Weber's own definition is even more structural: ' "Economic chances" shall be called chances promised by custom, interest position or (conventionally or legally) guaranteed order with respect to an economy.'[28] More specifically, Weber clearly implies that economic chances are themselves scarce so that one has to compete for them. Weber is imaginative in finding names for such chances, and we have mentioned some of them already:

market chances, chances of acquisition, exchange chances, price chances, supply chances, interest chances, work utilization chances, capital formation chances. 'Social chances' are treated by Weber in an analogous manner, so that he speaks of the 'estate chances' which go with certain kinds of skilled labour, and which are probabilities of the satisfaction of needs and wants arising from a person's position in fields of social relations. It is no longer surprising then that for Weber gods have chances too, including 'the chance of a god to conquer for himself primacy in the pantheon and eventually the monopoly of divinity.'[29] People hope to find by religion an 'improvement of their chances of rebirth',[30] or at any rate 'new future chances'.[31]

Multiplying the concept in this way does not yield much for analysis, of course. The next question is: What are the structural conditions of the probability of satisfying interests and needs which is intended by the objective concept of chance? For Weber, this is the question of law and authority (power). 'Appropriated chances shall be called "rights",' Weber says in a statement which we have already quoted and which he repeats. Thus rights are appropriated chances. In this context, property ('appropriated') is on the one hand a metaphor indicating the presence of an entitlement, thus of a guarantee. Rights are chances open to litigation. On the other hand, the property metaphor emphasizes that chances, even if they are guaranteed by law and anchored in complex structures, are always the chances of individuals, in whatever role or capacity they may appear. In any event, legal norms are, for Weber, a special case of social chances, characterized by the fact that they are integrated or doubly objective by being secured through sanctions.

For sociological analysis, rights are not suspended in mid-air. In a normative (Weber would say juridical) context it would suffice to tie rights to basic rights, natural rights, evident or divine norms: but the sociologist is interested in the origin, decay and change of rights in society. This means that people can dispose of rights, as of chances in general: or put differently, rights call for an organization that is capable of codifying and dispensing them.[32] Rights guaranteed by solidary groups create 'estates' which involve not only 'estate chances' but also the potential of organizing such chances and administering them: 'Any firm appropriation of chances, especially chances of domination, tends to lead to the formation of estates. Any formation of estates tends to lead to the monopolistic appropriation of powers of domination and chances of acquisition.'[33] Associations dispose of chances and thereby influence those special chances which are called rights. Parties are defined by the fact that they 'attribute power to their leaders within an association and thus (ideal or material) chances (of realizing substantive goals or achieving personal goals or both) to their active members'.[34] And rights are, 'sociologically speaking: the chance of support by the apparatus of force of the state for powers of command'.[35]

Even without discussing Weber's concepts of norm, legitimacy, power and authority in any detail, two of his definitions must be introduced here. One is almost too familiar to repeat:

> Power means any chance to realize one's own will, within a social relationship, even against resistance, whatever this chance is based on.
>
> Authority shall mean the chance to find obedience for a command of definite content with a defined set of persons. . . .[36]

In both definitions, chance is in the first instance no more than reasonable probability. What makes them reasonable, and indeed probable, however, has to do, in the case of authority, with the existence of rights or of law which we have already encountered. Authority is not simply 'any kind of chance to exercise "power" or "influence" over other people',[37] but it requires legitimacy. (Characteristically, and misleadingly, Weber abandons structural analysis here and tends to reduce legitimacy to believed legitimacy, indeed the belief in legitimacy. In our context, the following statement is particularly telling: 'The "legitimacy" of an authority must of course equally be regarded as a mere chance to be considered and treated as such to a relevant extent.'[38] In a sense, this provides the –

shaky – bridge from objective to subjective chances.) However, legitimacy, or legitimate validity, requires the factual orientation towards norms of legitimacy, and thus an element of that social structure which provides the foundation of chances.

The other definition which is relevant in this context takes us very close to the complete concept of life chances with which we are concerned. Command over chances, authority and its absence, constitute social facts of determining importance for the life of the individual as well as for estates and classes.

'Class position' shall mean the typical chance: 1. of supply of goods, 2. of external position in life, 3. of internal destiny in life, which arises from extent and kind of command power (or its absence) over goods or achieved qualifications and from the given manner of its utility for attaining a wage or an income within a given economic order.[39]

The concept is almost frighteningly catholic; for once one has listed both the 'external position in life' and the 'internal destiny of life', thus occupation and temperament, one needs hardly add the 'supply of goods'. Others would define class position as the typical chance of controlling means of production, or even as the typical chance of exercising power. However that may be, Weber gives us here a comprehensive concept to describe people's position in social life (although he got no further in developing the concept than Marx did in his unfinished chapter on class.) Characteristically, the concept reappears in the definition of what Weber calls 'struggle', or conflict, that is, the social relation in which 'action is oriented to the intention of realizing one's own will against the resistance of the partner or partners'.[40] This is where Weber introduces the notion of 'selection' as a form of struggle:

We shall call 'selection' the (latent) struggle for existence of human individuals or types for life chances or chances of survival which takes place without any meaningful intention of conflict: 'social selection' insofar as the chances of living people in life, 'biological selection' insofar as the chances of survival of genes are concerned.[41]

A trace of the social darwinism of his time is unmistakable in these statements of Weber's. The notion of 'survival chances' is immediately linked with genetic selection, and where he refers, a little later, to the 'struggle of the individual for life and survival chances', and to the '(latent) selection with respect to life and survival chances',[42] there remains a slight doubt whether this is a social category at all. Still, we can take it that in answering the question of what certain kinds of conflict are about, Weber introduces chances, or reasonable probabilities of survival and of life. What this might mean becomes a little clearer as Weber proceeds to describe the process of the formation of society as leading to 'a differentiation of the life and survival chances created by it'.[43] Here, one may suspect a version of the wider concept of class position; though the following statement casts doubt on this assumption:

And any order of social action, whatever it is like, somehow leaves unaffected the pure factual selection in the competition of different human types for life chances.[44]

It must remain open whether 'life chances' in this context refers to the sum total of specific (objective) chances which are appropriated to an individual under given social conditions, or whether it has to be seen along with all other chances to describe biological probabilities of development emerging from social structures.

Finally, there is one other place in the first volume of *Economy and Society* which is important in our context. Weber refers to the 'decisive motive force for all economic action', and thus for a central area of social action.[45] He differentiates with respect to this motive force. For those who have no property it is the supply of basic goods. For those who are 'in fact privileged' by virtue of their property or education, the emphasis is on 'chances of privileged earned income' apart from certain value preferences. What matters for owners, apart from economic considerations, is 'autonomous control ... over vital cultural and practical supply chances of an indeterminate plurality: power'. Vital cultural and practical supply chances, however, are in fact a central sector of social life chances, even if Weber chooses not to use the concept here.

The salad of chances made up by these quotations is rather mixed and possibly confusing. First of all, it provides an illustration of the fact that *Economy and Society* is a giant quarry in which many a mineral may still be found. It shows, moreover, that Max Weber had a considerable predilection for the word and the concept of chance without ever trying to define it systematically. If one were to define it generally, two features would deserve emphasis. One is that for Weber chances describe probabilities of the empirical occurrence of events. This is what is meant by the nominalist reservation in Weber's thinking, although it is in fact more than mere nominalism.

For the other feature is that such probabilities are not merely based on the empirical generalization of observations, but are in each case based on specific 'facts', on elements of social structure. It is only a small step from this approach to the statement that social structures are arrangements of chances. This raises for Weber, and beyond him, the question of what is meant by social structure. We cannot pursue the question here apart from one detail which is as important for Max Weber's concept of chance as it is for understanding life chances in general.

Social structures are always structures of social norms, the validity of which is guaranteed by second-order norms or sanctions. (Again it is apparent here how central the category of power is in the catalogue of basic sociological concepts.) Structures can be analyzed as such, as one can analyze laws for example, though one cannot derive more from them than the probability – the 'chance' – of factual behaviour. The fact that people do not always behave in accordance with structural patterns means among other things that they do not necessarily know the expectations which govern their behaviour. Again it is useful to consider laws as an example. This is the truth in the much-discussed notion of 'objective interests' ('class interests') of which people become aware only under certain specified circumstances. Analogously, it would be possible to suggest an analysis of structural opportunities of individual development –

in this sense of life chances – without assuming that people necessarily know the function of options and ligatures characteristic of their social position. It is quite misleading to distinguish in this context between objective and subjective dimensions; what matters is the distinction between structure and behaviour, opportunity and action, expectation and reality, pattern and fact, welfare chances and welfare, life chances and life.

But this is a note within a note, as it were. We have seen that 'chance', for Max Weber, has a dual meaning. In many places, he uses the term to describe the probability of people behaving in certain ways. We have neglected this branch of meaning here. For another one is more fruitful in that it describes chance as the crystallized probability of finding satisfaction for interests, wants and needs, thus the probability of the occurrence of events which bring about such satisfaction. The interests, needs and wants in question may be of many kinds: supply of goods, a pension, the acquisition or exchange of commodities, affiliation to an estate, a preferential social position, a position of power, indeed rebirth and the hope for a new future.

If one follows up the structures on which the probability of the satisfaction of such interests, wants and needs is based, one opens the door to the central areas of sociological analysis, the theories of norms and laws, of power and authority. Justifiable chances, thus rights, and command over them, thus power, and the struggle for legitimate command chances are but a segment of the total field of social chances, but one which leads to the central issues: What is the motive force of the economy? What are social conflicts about? What is it therefore that is structured in human societies?

Max Weber does not use any single concept in order to answer these questions. Where he himself speaks of life chances, the notion remains ambiguous. The most comprehensive concept of social chances in his terminology is the one associated with 'class position'. Thus Weber's concept of 'chance' is in an important sense suggestive rather than conclusive, stimulating rather than fully developed. We have let ourselves be stimulated

and taken the concept further in order to show that a precise
and at the same time general concept of life chances is central
for social analysis: that it links sociological analysis and political
theory; and that the substance of the concept takes us at the
same time into the theory of history.

V Classificatory and Other Games

This much is unmistakable at this point of our deliberations: it
is easier to deal with life chances either in the rigour of abstrac-
tion or in the randomness of lyrical watercolours than to define
and operationalize the concept and its elements. We shall not
be able to remedy this deficiency here in a satisfactory manner;
but it may be helpful to give a few indications. Let us start with
the elements of life chances.

Ligatures (linkages, bonds) are characterized by the fact that
they relate people to an anchorage which transcends special
social relations and power decisions and escapes rapid historical
change, the relation itself being naturally subject to change in
long historical rhythms. A simple classification might com-
mence with the dimensions of space and time. Space generally:
nature; space in a more limited sense: nation; space in the narrow
sense: region, landscape, community; social space: local community, family. Time generally: 'life'; time in a more limited
sense: history; time in the narrow sense: age, range of experience ('generation'); social time: 'social construction of human
life'. This is not a complete classification; the subject of religion
appears only indirectly. Still, the catalogue indicates the subjects of social ligatures.

Ligatures are themselves socially structured. Experience of
nature meant something different in the period of romanticism
from that of the renaissance. The meaning of age varies in
history. The attempt to operationalize the concept of life
chances is concerned with these social variants only insofar as
they provide examples. For example, the social construction of
human life is a kind of basic ligature, perhaps the backbone of

man's social existence: the relationship of social origin, education, work, leisure time and old age, to use the familiar categories of contemporary societies. One might identify a few other
basic ligatures, although their selection remains somewhat
arbitrary: religion, the social contract (with its ob*ligations*),
awareness of history, patriotism, sense of family.

If one considers measures for ligatures, their number is less
important than their intensity. (There is also the much more
difficult, yet central question of quality: the difference between
the devout Catholic and the Peoples' Temple fanatic, or between the chauvinist and the patriot. Social science is silent
here, although the social scientist must not remain silent.)[46]
One might establish a list fashioned on the one above and
determine the intensity of ligatures both within categories and
for all of them together in the terms of both particular social
positions and people with all their positions, indeed groups and
societies. The discussion of 'anomie' (vi, below) provides an
example of application to the analysis of total societies.

While ligatures fasten social positions, and people as their
incumbents, in social space, options create an – in principle
unlimited – arsenal of variations of behaviour. Ligatures are
given, options are wanted. They too could be classified in the
categories of space and time: as alternatives of movement in
space and alternatives of control over time. Indeed, independence with respect to time and room for manoeuvre in space,
thus chances of disposition and chances of mobility are two basic
figures of social options; it is no accident that both are frequently
identified with 'freedom'. If one is 'master of one's affairs', one
has a high measure of options.

By contrast to ligatures, options can be classified instru-
mentally as well (unless one wants to describe 'faith, love and
hope' as instruments for the creation of ligatures). We have
referred earlier to the philosophy of money; whatever the
limitations of the financial cynicism may be, in modern
societies money is certainly an instrument of social options. This
is true also, and in all known societies, for two other (connected)
forces, power (authority) and the law. Among these, power

(authority) has a special position in that it is always in control of the life chances of others, while it may well restrict the options of the incumbent.

The reasonable assumption that options should be quantifiable for positions, persons, groups and societies has led to a tendency to try to translate all options into one dimension. This is of course the implicit significance of gross national product and per capita income. Mobility, too, is occasionally used as a preferred measure of options. The same is true for power and authority ('he can do what he wants'). I confess that I find it easier to criticize such attempts than to put a better one in their place.

We have defined life chances as functions of ligatures and options. In an abstract sense, this statement is clear enough: $LC = f(L,O)$, perhaps even $LC = L \cdot O$. We have hinted at examples: the society in which people's lives are entirely linkage without choice is as bare of life chances as is the other extreme in which lives are entirely choice without linkage. In between the two, there are numerous, indeed in principle infinite possibilities. If one assumes a scale of coordinates extending from o to 1, one can see, for example, that the combination of options of 1 with ligatures of ·1 covers a much smaller sector (of life chances) than the combination of options of ·5 with ligatures of ·5. In this way, the idea of an optimal relation between options and ligatures can be expressed in quantitative terms.

This is, however, a pseudo-quantitative method which has many preconditions that have yet to be demonstrated. It presupposes, for example, that it is possible to measure both options and ligatures on one-dimensional scales. At the present stage of intellectual and technical development, it makes much more sense to work with aggregate concepts which appear less precise, but have more substance. Adam Smith for example (and similarly John Stuart Mill) speaks in his *Wealth of Nations* of the 'natural progress of opulence' and distinguishes three stages or levels of such welfare chances: 'subsistence', 'conveniency' and 'luxury'.[47] The disadvantage of this classification is that it overemphasizes the aspect of options; we shall see that this is true for all classifications which aim at quantification; but it does provide a beginning.

If one wants to adopt a scheme of three layers, one can identify first of all survival chances: their elements are (at least) the obligations of the social contract and the welfare chances of a subsistence minimum. Survival chances offer elementary security. At a next stage, there are the chances of a good life, chances of prosperity or, with Smith, conveniency perhaps; they include religion and law as well as a considerable level of welfare and complex institutions. Exceptional or privileged chances, luxury chances perhaps, entail on the other hand the highest level of options and ligatures attainable at a given time, thus subtle linkages which the individual has creatively appropriated by understanding and activity, coupled with a barely restricted command over time and space. (Here, one approaches almost automatically Aristotle's 'theoretical life', about which more will be said in the chapter on 'representative activities'.)

The classification contains no assumption about necessary progress and indicates possible directions rather than destinations of change even where it contains evident value judgments. Numerous statements about such directions of change can be made: from the social contract through the creation of the minimal state on to the rule of law and the democratic rule of law; from a *per capita* income of $100 through one of $1,000 to one of $10,000; from an imprecise mythological understanding of history through memory over three generations further to sophisticated historical awareness. . . . The temptation is too great, however, to put together endless chains of 'progress' where all that we wanted to do is to indicate possibilities of classification.

In introducing the concept of life chances, we have indicated somewhat informally on several occasions three developmental categories which are worth pursuing: the *emergence* of life chances, their *enhancement* or development and their *extension*.

Emergence is of course a key process for our understanding of history. History is open, insofar as the possibility of the emergence of new things exists. Let us take education as an example of the emergence of a new life chance. We shall understand by education the process of forming the individual by confronting him, usually in institutions, with the skills and values of his time through the formative capacity of his elders. This life chance emerges (a process, incidentally, which is more immediately plausible with respect to life chances of a technological or even legal character) in an abstract sense by its invention. New life chances are thought up for the first time by someone somewhere; this is indeed the basis for the representative function of certain human activities. In the case of education, this may have been (or so we shall assume for the purposes of this argument) Plato by his idea of the Academy. One must include the first realization of an idea in the process of its emergence; what actually happens in one place is by the same token more than merely possible. The foundation of the Academy documents the fact that education as a life chance has emerged.

A second, qualitatively different, though immensely important process is the enhancement or development of existing life chances. We speak of the development of the concept of education (if we are interested in intellectual history), or that of curricula, or of educational institutions. These are processes which fall into Kant's somewhat restrictive category of progress; they are the unfolding of a pattern. We must realize that almost everything which any one generation experiences in its social environment is development or enhancement rather than emergence. The genuinely new is rare; in order to recognize it at all, it is well to remember Popper's saying that there was no poetry in the lemur. As a continuing process, however, enhancement or development can come quite close to emergence. The difference between the education which Thomas Hobbes gave the young Earl of Devonshire and education in the sense of the *Ecole Normale* is considerable. Again, technology provides even more striking examples of the development of chances leading right up to the boundary of emergence.

Then there is the process of extension. It consists in making life chances which have been invented and developed available to more people. The thesis that education is a civil right requires the extension of education to the greatest possible number of people. This is not the place to discuss the problems (notably the paradoxes of Hirsch) which arise in this context.

All three dimensions of change in the social household of life chances permit their own analysis and, in principle, quantification.

It must be noted at least that a simple classification of 'institutional orders' – with or without the theoretical claims of Gerth and Mills[48] – is of course quite suitable for drawing up a catalogue of life chances: life chances of kinship, political life chances, economic life chances, military life chances, religious life chances. Evidently, a classification of this kind cannot solve the problems which we are discussing in this chapter; questions of measurement, of historical stages, of the interrelations of options and ligatures remain. But they help focus on specific issues. This is where what Merton himself calls the analysis of 'economic life chances' becomes relevant.[49] A special treatise could be written about political life chances which would cast new light on the genealogy of forms of government; in this way, one might even find a yardstick for evaluating the contrast between representative government and participatory democracy.

As we refer to the measurement of what human societies are about, the 'social indicators movement' (as it unfortunately calls itself) must not be overlooked. It arises out of the insufficiency of traditional economic measures and supplements these by aspects of the quality of life on the one hand, and by perceived welfare ('happiness') on the other. Eric Allardt has constructed a fourfold table of 'dimensions of welfare' in which he distinguishes on one axis objective welfare and happiness, and on the other elementary conditions of life and quality of life.[50] The much-discussed OECD programme of social indicators lists nine goal areas with several aspects each: they include objective indicators like 'personal income and wealth' or 'rule of law', new semi-objective indicators like 'quality of working life' and 'primary and secondary social allegiances', and more clearly subjective indicators like 'learning satisfaction' or 'confidence in the legal system'.[51] Wolfgang Zapf has constructed more systematic matrices of welfare components and has thereby given the combined subjective-objective approach a certain theoretical dignity.[52]

There is no need to repeat here the basic criticism of the limits of social indicators (cf. above, p. 34 sq.). It concerns above all the subjective aspects of indicators. If one takes this criticism into account, the development of subtle social indicators still remains a remarkable attempt to come to grips with theoretically relevant social objectives in the light of empirical possibilities. A measure of life chances (including 'income', 'rule of law' and 'social allegiances') is conceivable which, while not satisfying the theoretical claims of the concept of life chances, does not damage them either. The only question is whether for the time being, social indicators which are theoretically less ambitious might not be practically more useful.

Four-fold tables are a popular sport in the social sciences, though they are often more misleading than informative. Life chances provide a telling illustration. It would not seem implausible to begin by confining ourselves to making qualitative or simple quantitative ('bigger than . . .') statements about the life chances of given societies or social groups. For this purpose one would have to distinguish between conditions of smaller or larger options and weaker or stronger ligatures. The result would be a table in which we could enter, as examples, societies (countries), social groups and social roles.

But what do these various patterns of life chances tell us? More precisely: Where is the society with the greatest life chances, and where is that with the least life chances? Earlier remarks may have suggested a certain preference for Britain; but this is entirely idiosyncratic. The four-fold table is static. The most it can tell us is that as one moves away from its centre one also moves away from an optimum of life chances; this is no less true

OPTIONS

	small	large
strong	China traditional working-class monk	Britain traditional upper-class king
weak	Brazil 'modern youth drug addict	West Germany new middle-class pop star

LIGATURES

Figure 1. Life chances: example of a four-fold table

for the 'anomic' structures of 'modern youth' as it is for the immobility of the traditional working class. Beyond that the table does not tell us anything either about the quality of options and ligatures, or above all about the processes of development which make it possible to put something into one box rather than another: the 'strong' ligatures of Britain are incomparably weaker than those of China, and the 'small' options of 'modern youth' are incomparably larger than those of the traditional working class. Thus the four-fold table is all but useless.

On the other hand, one might transform the boxes of the table into points in a system of coordinates of options and ligatures. (We are doing this here in a playful way and on the assumption that both, options and ligatures, vary on a scale from 0 to 1.)

In this way it not only becomes possible to mark differences of distance between various positions, but one can also pose questions about processes of development: Are there fundamental patterns of development (e.g. modernity) which make it possible to identify variations in the progress of life chances as such?

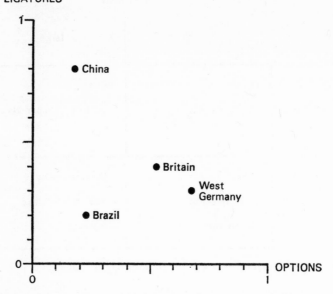

LIGATURES

China

Britain

West
Germany

Brazil

OPTIONS

Figure 2. Life chances: example of a system of coordinates

Are there typical break points in this process at which prevailing tendencies are arrested or reversed? Could it be that there are, if we take into account historical experience, several optimal points in the field of ligatures and options? The system of coordinates can do no more than stimulate such questions; answers remain limited by the information which has entered into its markings.

The four-fold table is static above all insofar as it does not enable us to express the simultaneous strengthening (not just strength) of both elements. If one introduces this time horizon, it becomes possible to make a distinction of considerable importance.

First, we can in principle measure the horizon of the life chances which are available at a given time in terms of that of later (or even earlier) times. Gaius Julius Caesar could not be a Christian, and Nero could not have a private aeroplane. There may well be large shifts of this horizon. Here, Marx's concept of productive forces might be relevant. The notion of a change of theme or subject from medieval hierarchy to modernity (and beyond) also becomes capable of definition in this way.

Secondly, the position of the individual (as well as that of groups and societies) in the horizon of the relevant time can be measured. Relations of production have a reference to forces of production, as do actual conditions to a potential.

In this way, the statement becomes understandable: 'My grandparents had everything one could possibly have, but I would not want to change places with them.' It appears understandable, at any rate, for one also recognizes complications. Let us take an example:

Time A has a horizon of 20 chances (out of 100);
X has 19 of 20 = 95 per cent.
Time B has a horizon of 40 chances (out of 100);
Xson has 30 of 40 = 75 per cent.

Here, the two statements about which many a book has been written become possible: 'Xson is better off than X, because he has more than 50 per cent more (19:30).' And: 'Xson is worse off than X, for he has only 75 per cent of what was possible in his time, whereas X had 95 per cent'. Many an idea, from nostalgia for happy primitives to pity for the relatively deprived, can be latched on to these observations.

Similar observations can of course be applied to less secular matters as well: the working man has 95 per cent of what his social stratum can offer him; the person who has risen socially from the working class has a mere 75 per cent of what his new stratum has to offer, though it is more than the status of the working man. There is no shortage of possibilities of complication which demonstrate the charms and the pitfalls of comparison.

Let us end the games. Their primary function in this context was to provide additional illustration. At the end there is little doubt that we still have a long way to go before we reach operational precision. Even at the level of conceptual discussion, enough questions remain. They concern above all the abstract distinction and conceptual combination of options and ligatures. Are large options and strong ligatures really conceivable at the same time? Is there not, on the other hand, a border area in which differences tend to be blurred, an area of 'freely chosen linkages'? And if one tries to think both, options and ligatures, together, do they combine into one complex, or do they remain separate elements like, say, income and civil rights? The proposal of a concept which is made in this volume is in the first instance no more than a proposal, although it may have a certain immediate plausibility.

VI On Social Structure and Anomie

On several occasions it has become apparent that in this conceptual discussion we are moving in a certain proximity to Durkheim's notion of anomie. The statement in particular that an increase of options may be accompanied by a decrease in life chances, if the weakening of ligatures goes too far, reminds one of this tradition of sociological analysis. It has been advanced above all by Robert Merton in his two essays on 'Social Structure and Anomie' which have justly become classics.[53] These essays, however, contain – as we shall try to show here – an ambiguity which can be resolved with the help of the concept of life chances. For strictly speaking, their subject is not the relation between social structure and anomie, but that between social structure and deviant behaviour.

Merton begins with a distinction. He separates 'culture goals' and the 'institutionalized means' which are needed in order to attain these goals; in the later essay he refers at one point to 'the cultural structure, on the one hand, and the social structure on the other'.[54] Both may be in harmony (as Merton points out above all in terms of the success theme in American society); then we have 'conformity'. But they may also fall apart in four different ways: the goals may be accepted, but the means rejected (*innovation*); the goals may be rejected, but the means accepted (*ritualism*); both goals and means may be rejected (*retreatism*); and retreatism may be turned into an active posture by demands for new goals and means (*rebellion*). In a strict sense, all four attitudes are kinds of deviant behaviour; on several occasions, Merton himself describes them as such.

But then Merton introduces the term anomie, and not only in the title of the first of the two essays. 'It is, indeed, my central hypothesis that aberrant behaviour may be regarded sociologically as a symptom of dissociation between culturally prescribed aspirations and socially structured avenues for realizing these aspirations.'[55] A little later, he identifies this very process with 'what Durkheim called "anomie" (or normlessness)'.[56] In the later essay, Merton defines a little more ambiguously: 'Anomie is then conceived as a breakdown in the cultural structure, occurring particularly when there is an acute disjunction between the cultural norms and goals and the socially structured capacities of members of the group to act in accord with them.'[57] The reticence of the statement ('particularly') and the correction of concepts ('breakdown in the cultural structure') deserve to be noted.

At the beginning of the later essay, Merton quotes the important definition of anomie given by MacIver. Its conceptual language has an evident connection with our own deliberations:

Anomy signifies the state of mind of one who has been pulled up by his moral *roots*, who has no longer any *standards*, but only *disconnected* urges, who has no longer any sense of *continuity*, of folk, of *obligation*. The anomic man has become spiritually sterile, responsive only to himself, *responsible* to no one. He derides the *values* of other men. His only *faith* is the philosophy of denial. He lives on the thin line of sensation between no future and no past. . . . Anomy is a state of mind in which the individual's sense of *social cohesion* – the mainspring of his *morale* – is broken or fatally weakened.[58]

The fact that we have emphasized in this quotation all those concepts which belong in the vocabulary of ligatures may betray the gist of our argument. Merton himself, in quoting

MacIver, has emphasized the phrase 'state of mind'; his argument is that MacIver's concept of anomie is psychological rather than sociological. Merton rightly emphasizes the need for a structural concept (and of appropriate measures for it, including 'improved measures of the still loosely-utilized but important concept of what Weber called "life-chances" in the opportunity-structure').[59] But one must doubt at least whether he was right to put MacIver's definition on one side as he set out to look for a 'social topography of anomie'.[60] For while MacIver refers to a state of mind, it is not difficult to extract the psychological elements from the concepts which he uses for its description; we have pursued a similar line many times as we were discussing ligatures.

If one is prepared to take this step, certain ambiguities in Merton's formulations become telling. There is a considerable difference between the distinction of 'cultural' as against 'social structure' on the one hand, and 'culture goals' as against 'institutionalized means' on the other. It is at least conceivable that the 'cultural structure' is the epitome of linkages which defy rapid changes and conscious interventions and determine the position of the individual. On the other hand, statements like this acquire a new meaning: 'The social structure acts as a barrier or as an open door to the acting out of cultural mandates.'[61] If we ignore the reference to 'cultural mandates' for the moment, the definition of social structure sounds almost like one of options: the cultural sphere determines the linkages in which people find themselves, whereas the sphere of society describes possibilities of choice for their action. American society emphasizes, by the predominance of the success theme the option dimension of social structure, while the dimension of linkages is given a secondary place. This is why there is in it (and in similar societies) a built-in strain towards anomie.

I do not want to take the reinterpretation of Merton's texts too far; it is in any case merely an instrument to help us understand the category with which we are concerned in this book. However, three conclusions of this interpretation may be useful for that purpose.

The first conclusion is that Merton's essays should be given a new title: 'Social Structure, Deviant Behaviour and Social Change'. Although they contain a number of references to the phenomenon of anomie, this is decidedly not their central subject; for the phenomenon which Merton has in mind, the name anomie is surprising. Cleavages between values and patterns of behaviour have as such little to do with anomie; they are, rather, a part of the theory of change.

This means, secondly, that anomie should be defined by the absence of linkages or ligatures, that is by the structural phenomena which give rise to the state of mind of which MacIver has given such a lively description. Anomie as the absence of linkages corresponds to a state of optionlessness with respect to the other dimension of life chances (although in fact it tends to occur in combination with an abundance of options). The consequences of this definition of the concept both for measuring anomie and for exploring its implications are evident.

Both these conclusions, however, are terminological and therefore secondary. The third conclusion resulting from them is substantively more important. Anomie is usually described as normlessness (a description suggested by the word itself, which contains the Greek word $\nu\acute{o}\mu os$). Thus it might appear as if societies (or the social position of particular groups, or even particular social positions) differed in the degree to which they are structured or have structure. It is certainly possible to use the term structure in this way; but if one did so, one would have to replace our concept of 'ligatures' by 'structures' and speak of a destructuring process instead of a weakening of ligatures. This in turn would make it necessary to find another concept which describes the fact that even in a society or situation in which linkages lose their effect there exist valid norms and sanctions, in this sense social structures. The concept of ligature achieves something which the concept of structure in its customary use cannot achieve: it indicates the effect of particular linkages and bonds. One might distinguish (for example) between simple and complex structures; but in terms of the notion to which we shall adhere here, intensity is not a useful

D

measure of structure. The fact that the effect of the rules of the Catholic church has decreased for the secularized Frenchman does not indicate a loss of structure, but a loss of linkage. The fact that the insistence of the Catholic church on conformity (the force of its sanctions) has decreased does not indicate a diminution, but a modification of structure, possibly an increase of options, although this is not necessarily accompanied by a weakening of ligatures. Thus we shall use structure as a concept which characterizes all societies and cannot meaningfully be discussed in terms of presence or absence. Whatever the dimensions are in which social structures vary, they exclude those which are characteristic for ligatures and options (the scale from o to 1). Structure is a general, totally neutral, in a sense colourless concept intended to describe and analyze social norms and sanctions as well as the positions, roles, interest groups etc. established by them.

For our present context this means above all that anomie is, so to speak, a false word. It is not the νόμοι, the structures and rules which disappear in that state which Durkheim, MacIver, and here and there even Merton have in mind, but the bonds and linkages, the ligatures. There is little point in trying to replace the familiar concept by a new one – aligie? or in using the Greek word δέσις, adesie? – but it would be useful to correct many a definition of what people have in mind when they speak of anomie.

VII Further on
Life Chances and Liberty

Life chances and liberty are not the same; but an exploration of the relation between the two may contribute to clarifying the notion of liberty. In doing so, we assume (first) that the concept of life chances is an analytical category whereas liberty is of necessity a normative concept; despite the fact that we have occasionally spoken of the 'greatest life chances of the greatest number', more life chances for more people are not necessarily a good thing, whereas he who wants liberty takes sides (from a certain point onwards, as we shall presently show). There is (secondly) a complication in the fact that while freedom means under all circumstances an extension of life chances, this statement could not be reversed. Improving the standard of living in the Soviet Union means an enhancement of life chances, but not an enhancement of liberty. This becomes understandable (thirdly), if we distinguish between liberties and liberty (some would say between liberty and freedom), that is, between the necessary and the sufficient conditions of liberty. The former describe a state of affairs in which certain life chances have to be given; the latter describe an attitude which may be defined as the untiring quest to extend life chances but which does not contain a list of necessary (indispensable) life chances.

This is a complicated idea, and we can but offer aphoristic explanations in this note.

'We are concerned in this book,' says Hayek in his *Constitution of Liberty*, 'with that condition of men in which coercion of some by others is reduced as much as is possible in society. This state we shall describe throughout as a state of liberty or freedom.'[62] We agree with this statement without reservation. All comments on this first principle of the necessary conditions of liberty in society serve to explain and supplement it; they must not be misunderstood as alibis for abuse, as secret escapes for tyrants. The necessary conditions of liberty are indeed the conditions of the open society. They include the basic liberties which emerge from the condition of uncertainty in which we are living: the possibility of change by institutions which allow the suggestion and realization of different designs for the future. This means the inviolability of the person, freedom of speech and of conviction, elementary political participation (and all this, as the case may be, in a more or less subtle and sophisticated form). Where the life chances indicated by these values are not given, there is no freedom, however high the standard of living of people may be. The necessary conditions of liberty are indispensable in the strict sense of the word.

It may be noted in this context that this elementary freedom presupposes the social contract (the 'minimal state'), and to that extent includes an element of coercion, or at least of constraint, of limitations placed on the theoretically unlimited possibilities of action.

With respect to the necessary conditions of liberty, it makes sense to speak of a 'state of liberty', although I prefer the expression 'necessary conditions'. Beyond these necessary conditions, however, it is dangerously misleading to refer to a 'state of liberty'. In the third volume of *Capital* there is the important place at which Marx distinguishes between the 'realm of freedom' and the 'realm of necessity'. Work, he argues, 'which is determined by need and external objectives' and thus constitutes the 'sphere of material production proper' can never be truly free, but 'always remains a realm of necessity. Beyond its boundaries that development of human forces begins which is a purpose in itself, the true realm of freedom, which however can blossom only on that realm of necessity as its basis'.[63] This argument would deserve a more extensive analysis than we can attempt here, if only because it expresses the common conviction of rulers and ruled in modern societies. For this conviction is wrong.

The proposition corresponds to a widespread experience. Work is disagreeable and will always be so; but since it is a mere instrument for attaining life chances, one must suffer it, make it as short and painless as possible and otherwise concentrate on areas which offer greater chances. This is what follows if one adopts a static (and therefore defeatist) notion of liberty! The possibility of turning an apparently instrumental area of human activity itself into a source of life chances is not even considered; it would follow that a programme for the 'humanization of work' is rejected from the outset. (In a more extensive analysis one could also support the argument that he who is prepared to renounce liberty in one realm of life is likely to lose it all in the end.) The attempt to push the claim of liberty right into the so-called realm of necessity may not belong to the necessary conditions of freedom, but it is characteristic of its sufficient conditions, thus of the untiring quest for an extension of life chances, especially in places in which this may seem improbable at first sight.

The abolition of poverty is a sufficient, not a necessary condition of liberty. Indian voters have realized this more clearly when they cast their vote in 1977 than all theorists of 'freedom from need' who are prepared to balance poverty and misery against elementary liberties.

What we have called the necessary conditions of liberty here includes a strict, well-defined combination of options and ligatures: the social contract plus freedom of speech, so to speak, thus the fundamental linkages of all society coupled with respect for the fundamental opportunities for choice of the irrepressible human individual. This basic set of liberal life chances could be described with great precision; it is, so to say, the first table of liberal politics which one must never lose sight of and always carry around with one, even if one hopes to live under conditions which make it unnecessary ever to cite this particular text.

Hayek defends himself against the charge that his concept of liberty is 'purely negative': 'It becomes positive only through what we make of it. It does not assure us of any particular opportunities, but leaves it to us to decide what use we shall make of the circumstances in which we find ourselves.'[64] Nowhere is the deeply conservative bent of a concept of liberty which is confined to its necessary conditions more evident. I hasten to add that there are worse things than the self-restraint of the liberal conservative: 'to live and let live' is not the worst maxim. But it is far from being the best. The 'circumstances in which we find ourselves' define as a constant the very things which are variable. Liberty in this case is no more than the implementation of the life chances which are available here and now. But there are other fetters on human development. That which we do not (yet) know or are not (yet) able to do is a limitation of what we know and do which can be removed. Satisfaction may be a desirable state of mind; but self-satisfaction and the inactivity which flows from it cannot be desirable in an imperfect world. The classical liberal concept of liberty is negative because it seems to be resigned to, indeed pleased with existing conditions.

The invitation for change which characterizes the active concept of liberty must not be misunderstood in quantitative terms. We are not referring here to the quest for more of the same thing. There was a social construction of human lives which consisted merely (for those who lived long enough) of a disciplined childhood, the endless 'realm of necessity', and old age. Today there is a social construction of human lives which consists of the mild morning mist of childhood, the stage of education or training, the parallel stages of work and leisure, the stage of active retirement, and the dusk of old age. There might be a social construction of human lives which recognizes much more flexible and variable combinations of work, education and leisure between childhood and old age, and which, in addition, makes them all as rich in chances (as free?) as possible. It is thus more important to explore new things than to amass those which are already there.

Easy as it may be to define the basic elements of the necessary conditions of liberty, it is difficult to do the same for the sufficient conditions. Both elements of life chances turn out to be somewhat awkward here.

So far as ligatures are concerned, this is easy to see. The social contract is a condition of the possibility of liberty; but what we have got used to calling law and order may turn into a condition of illiberty. Thus if the demand for legal and judicial linkages reaches a point at which only the most ready conformists do not suffer considerable restrictions of their behaviour, ligatures become a danger for liberty. It may well be true in any case that the more explicit ligatures are, the less liberty they permit. In the nature of the case, linkages and bonds should work without written rules and organized instances. While the church, the nation state, school curricula of history and the contract of marriage may be necessary, they are also the first step on the road to that alienation which robs linkages of their very essence. Decreed ligatures are in any case signs of illiberty; this is one of the reasons why the emergence and creation of ligatures is such a precarious process.

Perhaps we have exaggerated the dangers of options somewhat in these deliberations. In view of the limitations on human opportunities of choice in nearly all societies it is more important to break them than to praise them. We must not forget either that extending options is a complicated process which – as the development of citizenship rights shows by way of a *pars pro toto* – does not end with the promise of rights, but merely begins with it. People's standard of living, and their social status generally, are important as a real condition of options. Even in the most advanced societies, the process of opening up options for more people is quite incomplete. Yet the first signs of a kind of nausea may be noticeable, a shocked sense of a 'freedom to die', an abundance of opportunities. Certain kinds of competition for consumers in the market economies are one example, the horizon of life of fifteen to sixteen-year olds is a more serious one. There are in fact situations in which a reduction of options enhances life chances. People are more likely to grow by an 'I had to do it, but I . . . ', than by an 'I didn't know what to do, and then I. . . .'

We shall discuss liberal politics in the following chapters. Their principles, however, follow from these theoretical reflections. If liberty beyond the basics (the necessary conditions) is the impatient quest for new life chances for more people (as a sufficient condition), then the three elements of innovation become important here: the emergence, enhancement or development, and extension of life chances.

So far as the emergence of new life chances, their invention and first realization is concerned, it is apparent here that bringing about and securing the conditions of creative activity is an elementary requirement of liberty. Representative activities are no luxury. A society loses liberty not merely by silencing unwelcome views and the work of innovators, but also by ceasing to support the arts and the sciences. Uncomfortable authors need not be loved and pampered, but tolerating them is only a first step; there is much to be said for the Villa Massimo and the Institute of Advanced Study.

The enhancement or development of life chances as a task of liberty is the full realization of the potential of a society. This is easily said, but in practice it is quite difficult. Here too it should be emphasized that full realization does not simply mean more of the same thing. For a long time, the development of life chances in modern societies meant above all the development of options, for example, of civil rights. In many countries, and at some points of all societies, this is still a task of high priority. But it might well be – if the analysis at which we have hinted here without ever following it up is at all correct – that today the development of life chances in some areas of advanced societies means above all the growth of new ligatures, so that the greater danger to liberty arises not from the lack of options, but from that of linkages and bonds. The liberal programme which follows from this kind of observation has yet to be written.

The extension of life chances is not a simple process either. The notion of extension ('greatest chances of the greatest number') entails a demand for equality. At first sight, there is no reason to deprive anyone of life chances once they have emerged and been developed. As so often happens, however, a second look reveals complexities. The extension of the life chance university degree to fifty per cent of each age group destroys the chance itself. We need a more sophisticated concept of extension; one, moreover, which takes into account that some life chances defy extension and generalization. Here too we shall stop short of empirical analysis (although the following chapters will cross the boundary here and there) and confine ourselves to the assumption that for many equality is a condition of liberty, but that there are situations in which it threatens to destroy liberty. When and where this is the case, liberty has primacy. This may even turn – as we shall see in the chapter on 'Inequality, Hope and Progress' – into an argument in favour of inequality.

All foreign policy has one objective: peace. A foreign policy which is not serving peace is in itself evil. But it would be erroneous to believe that all domestic policy has one common objective as well, such as liberty. It is true that those basics, which we have described here as the necessary condition of liberty, make sense only if they are generally accepted; they become a partisan demand only under conditions of fundamental illiberty. (In our own century, there have been only too many occasions when this was the case.) Active liberty, however, that is the quest for more life chances for more people, is an objective which one might well dispute. There is a strictly conservative position which (with Hayek) advises people to rest content with the life chances which they have got already. The assertion that liberty is sufficiently defined by its necessary conditions belongs in this chapter. There is, on the other hand, a progressive position which regards it as possible and at times necessary to restrict the basic elements of liberty in order to extend the horizon of life chances. The dictatorship of the proletariat as a precondition of socialism provides an extreme, but by no means a unique example of this attitude. For the liberal, what I have called the basics of liberty are indispensable under all conditions, and change is invariably judged in terms of its capacity for opening up new life chances without destroying those already there. To that extent at least, liberty is a partisan programme even in a free society.

4 Liberalism

Anarchy is fine, but not very practical. If one thinks through the notion of equal life chances for all, one ends up almost inevitably with the concept of a society in which the power of men over men has been abolished; but if one thinks through the notion of a society without power, one will have to conclude (with Hobbes, or somewhat more cautiously, with Locke) that 'civil government is the proper remedy for the inconveniences of the state of nature'.[1] The way people are made, any kind of society requires certain rules which in turn must be backed up by sanctions; a 'minimal state' is unavoidable. The way people are made, however, these rules and the instances backing them up may be in error; they have to remain open to change for that reason. The possibility of progress is a condition of the battle against error. Thus we have almost defined liberalism: misanthropy plus hope; the attempt to link the practical necessity of power as intimately as possible with the greatest life chances of the greatest number; faith in the strength and the right of the individual, tempered by doubt in the perfection of things human; a little morals and a little epistemology.

The difference between liberalism thus defined and either pure conservatism, or progressivist doctrines of salvation, is evident. If the conservative accepts change at all, he has to regard it as an organic and marginal process outside the boundaries of human direction; the progressivist, on the other hand, advances a dangerously absolute claim in his programmatic rhetoric; and both in their ways have a curious preference for social collectivities, the estate, the nation, the family, the class, the people. There is an extreme version of such approaches, fascism, which is at the opposite end of the scale of political attitudes from liberalism. The moral element of liberal thought is the conviction that it is the individual that matters, and the defence of his inviolability, of the unfolding of his potential, of his life chances which follows from this conviction. Groups, organizations, institutions are never a purpose in themselves, they are instruments for the purpose of individual development. The individual, with his interests and dreams and desires, is also the motive force of social development. Thus society must above all create room for individual manoeuvre, it must set free forces which are in the end bound to be the forces that strengthen individual human beings. In this connection, notions like the rule of law and the market economy are important. But the individualism of the liberal has its meaning only in the context of the epistemological assumption that nobody knows all answers, or rather, that there can be no certainty about the truth or falsehood of given answers. We are living in a horizon of fundamental uncertainty. Such doubts in the absolute give rise to the demand for social and political conditions in which different answers can be given, both at a given point of time and over time; this is the condition of the open society. In this connection, the interest in freedom of expression and in political institutions which allow change, in democracy, are important.

So much for the pure doctrine. It is not to be dismissed, precisely because so many have identified 'liberals' with historical positions which have long since lost their significance. So many have called themselves liberals in history, free traders and nationalists, defenders of private property and enemies of the church, libertinists, people without a particular point of view, not to say opportunists, friends of big ideas and others who sought to camouflage their lack of ideas by big words. The main stream of liberal politics has itself been subject to many a change; it is no accident that the history of liberal parties is, in some countries, a history of splits and turns. The picture today is confusing: in Australia the conservatives call themselves Liberals, in Canada the social democrats; in Italy the Liberal Party has clung to an older liberalism of privilege and established power until its very existence was threatened, in the Federal Republic the Free Democratic Party has negotiated the curve into modernity at breakneck speed, in Denmark and elsewhere their momentum has carried the liberals out of this bend and turned them into teachers' and students' parties. Reality, in other words, offers barely a starting point of analysis, and recourse to pure doctrine makes sense, although it confirms Hayek's scepticism according to which liberalism is ('for the time being', as he is kind enough to say) 'more an intellectual than a political movement'.[2]

Developed societies (and they alone are our subject here) are faced with two collectivist threats. One is the conservative-authoritarian movement by way of law-and-order slogans back to an organized society modern-style; the other is a revolutionary-socialist movement by way of slogans of taxation and investment direction to a terrorist equality which George Orwell has described in a definitive manner. Whether a liberal position has a chance at all in the face of these dangers depends on two things: on the ability of liberals to apply their principles in a new way to a changed socio-economic climate, and on certain social and political developments which liberals themselves can only partly control. Let us look at both a little more closely.

An economy based on private property and competition is an undisputed mark of, at any rate, traditional European liberalism. These objectives are inspired by the hope that it may be possible to satisfy growing human wants and needs without force. The evidence is overwhelming that no other economic system has ever been as effective in achieving this as the liberal system. If they were free to choose, most people in the world would wish to live in countries like the United States and Canada, Australia, Germany and Britain. However, in the process of its success the liberal market economy has changed; indeed it demonstrates how yesterday's rules of the game may become today's fetters. A market economy aims at growth by the independent activity of many; but from a certain point onwards these two elements begin to contradict each other. The growth of production requires economic units (at least in certain branches) which no longer compete with others of a similar

kind, including in important areas the 'public sector', the
state; growth of real income, on the other hand, requires organizations which, like the trades unions, exploit their monopoly
position. In the face of such developments, a neo-liberal theory
à la Friedman is positively idyllic, and even institutions like the
anti-trust laws of the United States, cartel legislation in the
Federal Republic, and the competition policy of the European
Community are no more than rearguard actions. The reality of
modern economies is a system of mixed private-public property
and oligocentric structures of decision.

Under these circumstances, the mere repetition of yesterday's
liberal articles of faith may well become an alibi for leaving the
powerful of today uncontrolled: competition rules in fact become rules which enable the big to dictate their interests to all
others; collective bargaining rules in fact turn into rules which
enable the organized to establish their interests as the deter-
minant of the living conditions of all. Many liberals have not
yet recognized this new situation. As a result, they are in danger
of becoming the spokesmen of secondary branches of the
economy in which variants of the classical market theory may
still work, and of ignoring in the process the crucial question of
how one applies liberal principles under conditions of high
concentration, high organization and reduced expectations of
growth.

This is a dual question: How can the actions of the *nouveaux
riches* of power be controlled as effectively as those of democratic
governments? And is it possible to change the theme of economic
activity and replace naive expectations of growth by the improvement of human life? The questions hint at the direction in
which answers may be found. Wherever patterns of market
economy continue to be possible, they should be preserved,
strengthened, perhaps re-constituted. But in the key areas in
which this would be an illusion, the corrupt government of
public monopolies and cartels is as unsatisfactory as the secret
government of those in the private sector, especially since neither
likes to divulge its intentions to the other or to the public.
Democratization, decentralization, co-determination, and poli-

tical definition of certain economic guidelines are all objectives which make sense only if they are coupled with some reticence in the full exploitation of opportunities for growth (in traditional GNP terms): from an economy of thoughtless expansion to an economy of good housekeeping. This means of course that the marriage of liberalism and capitalism has to be dissolved.

The social process of developed countries reveals a figure of change which is analogous to that of the economic process. The liberation of a new potential by modernization, symbolized in the French Revolution, has meant unheard-of progress of life chances for many people. This was a dynamic process which began with the rule of law, that is, the protected formal status of the citizen, and ended with the welfare state, that is, comprehensive and substantive citizenship rights. Understandably and yet unfortunately, liberals have actually found this process painful. Their preference for the traditional minimal state has made them overlook for a long time the fact that the great revolution of the fundamental equality of status of all citizens and of universal suffrage had to remain incomplete without the civil right to assistance in need, the civil right to employment and a minimal income, the civil right to an education and other social rights. Some liberal parties have been panting breathlessly after the social-policy train of the times, only to reach it – like the German Free Democrats in their Freiburg programme of 1971 – when the train had already left the liberal destination: in trying to reconcile themselves with history, they are losing the present.

Today, social policy has often become a costly instrument of immobility. Worse still, the dynamics of equality has increasingly tended to blur the boundary between the necessary equality of opportunities and a discouraging equality of actual conditions; extreme forms of progressive taxation and misguided notions of comprehensive schools provide topical examples. Bureaucratization on the one hand, and social levelling on the other, are challenges to a liberal social policy which respects the achievements of the welfare state but never tires in its insistence that these achievements are about giving the individual more life chances, and that means an optimal combination of ligatures or bonds and room for manoeuvre or options. In the secular dialectics of liberty and equality, the hour of liberty has come, because it is threatened by a false egalitarianism. To this extent, the alliance of liberalism and socialism has exhausted its utility.

The interest and the merits of liberalism are most clearly evident in a third realm of politics, concern with constitutional arrangements. Democracy and the rule of law, and their joint development, are a liberal achievement. Insofar as there has been development, this concerned above all the rights of the individual. The legal and judicial systems provide numerous examples, from legal aid and prisoners' rights to de-regulation in areas of moral, but not of public, concern. Liberals, however, have little to say about new threats to parliamentary democracy, and have often confined themselves to reiterating the pure doctrine: demanding the abolition of 'grey areas' in which organizations and associations operate; encouraging shareholders to control enterprises more actively; showing sympathy for community politics and other forms of participation, including referenda, electoral reform and the like. But this is not enough. The 'structural change of the public'[3] in developed societies is so fundamental that the old litanies of representative democracy become either illusions or empty words. One aspect of this structural change is the change in political spaces. Multinational enterprises are not alone in the discovery of international, indeed supranational, spaces. The creation of effective checks and balances for the exercise of power in such wider spaces is a liberal desideratum of the first order, and one in which simple solutions (like direct elections to the European Parliament) are hardly sufficient. But simultaneously with a vast extension of political spaces we experience their shrinkage; civic participation in manageable spaces is a legitimate and agreeable result of the extension of citizenship rights, although such civic participation has yet to find adequate patterns.

Then there is the other part of the structural change of the public, its fragmentation, the 'new feudalism', the threat of the corporate state, the ossification of the political community by the neutralization of rival partial powers. Here, liberalism is challenged in its very principles, the defence of the individual and the demand for openness and change. Yet it would be an illusion to deduce from these principles the need for confrontation with the extra-parliamentary partial powers. Whoever sought this confrontation has lost it; Willy Brandt and Edward Heath are prominent examples. Individuals in developed societies are as a rule both individual citizens, voters who take their own decision in the polling booth, and members of organizations, employees of a firm, carriers of union cards, for whom the decisions of their firm and the successes of their union are in the end more important than the policies of their government. The task which emerges from such observations may look like squaring the circle; it is the creation of a new public which includes both individuals and organizations, and yet gives primacy to the general public of individuals; this is the unresolved main theme of a liberal approach to constitutional matters today. Dealing with this theme is not made easier by the fact that there are arguments for a new form of 'minimal state', for a kind of withering-away of the state, which must seem plausible to the liberal.[4]

The economic theorists of the second great growth period of modern history have called themselves neo-liberals. The liberal reformers of the late 1960s liked to describe themselves as 'social-liberals', with some wishing to go even further and call themselves 'radical-liberals'. The new liberty, which is the concern of liberalism in a changed climate, can only partly be described in such terms. It is a freedom from the constraints of a capitalist or socialist society bent on expansion, thus the freedom to improve the quality of individual lives in changed 'relations of production'. One might describe it as a programme for a liberal future.

But has liberalism got a future? Or, more precisely, has organized political liberalism got a future? And since announcements of the imminent demise of parties which allow themselves to be called liberal are likely to be as false in future as they were in the past, since we are therefore not concerned here with the Liberal Party of Great Britain, the Radikale Venstre, or the Freie Demokratische Partei, the question is: Will a programme for a liberal future be sufficiently attractive to sustain effective political organizations? This is the question of support for liberal positions, and the answer must surely be in doubt.

The changes in the socio-economic climate, of which some have been aware since the unilateral declaration of independence of the United States dollar in 1971, more since the so-called energy crisis of 1973, and nearly all since the stagflatory recession of 1973, have resulted in an astonishing renaissance of left and right conservatives. On the democratic left, this has taken the form of a defence of the welfare state against any kind of 'dismantling', coupled with a shift from the politics of reform to the politics of stability. Thus the left has become the conservative grouping in the strict sense of the word and no longer deserves the description, 'left'; we find here a 'social-democratic' consensus which extends far beyond the centre of the political spectrum. On the democratic right, which finds considerable social support, the process of a reversal of the trend continues all the way to nostalgia for premodern structures, including a little worry about employment as a stimulus for work ethics, the reduction of social services to the point which the community 'can afford', elements of social and political control which do not even stop short of freedom of the press, and general praise for the good old values of authority, discipline, order, punishment, and the like. While the left conservatism becomes an accepted general attitude, that of the right finds itself in a position of confrontation with prevailing conditions.

The same shift in context has moved the impatient reformers of the late 1960s to the fringe. They no longer influence the political process as did the allies of the May revolt in Paris in 1968 or those who voted for Brandt and Scheel in 1969, but they have become sectarians, conspirators, sometimes terrorists.

This changes the habitus, the pattern of organization, and the range of the spectrum of participation. Small groups of teachers and students which conquer local associations of parties, and may (as sometimes happens) be expelled, form their own little groups. They may frighten the majority of voters, but they do not determine the politics of their country. Since they become almost of necessity utopians and verbal revolutionaries, they dissociate themselves from liberals in the same rhythm.

In a situation like this, political liberalism is left essentially with two options. One is the organization of the 'thinking minorities', that is, those four, five, six per cent which doubt the value of big organizations under any circumstances; this would have to be combined with the hope for situational voters who at any one time do not want to make up their mind between equally suspicious alternatives. The room for manoeuvre of such an organization extends from less than five to almost twenty per cent in general elections; it may be decisive for political systems; but it has little to do with liberalism in an emphatic sense other than that it is an uncomfortable, healthy nuisance for others.

The other option is more complicated and much less interesting for the secretary general, let alone the leader of a party. People in modern societies are – fortunately – living complicated lives. They are trade-union members or belong to a church or object to the construction of a nuclear power station, and there are times when these concerns are more important for them than all others. These are times in which they vote for socialist or for Christian parties or opt for an extra-parliamentary opposition. But the same people are many other things as well: shop managers for example, supporters of Liverpool Football Club, young pop-music fans, caravan owners, board members of the local school, and in many other social roles. The same people have hopes and wishes of many kinds, not necessarily addressed to government, or even their firm or organization, but simply hopes for life chances. They do not create a new social problem. So far as their immediate things are concerned, they manage. But it is in their interest, and possibly in the interest of a free society of the future, that constellations are created in which these people's actions are not determined by just one of their social roles, so that they are not merely, or even primarily, church-goers or trade union members or opponents of nuclear power stations. One might, indeed, define the practical objective of a programme for a liberal future as the attempt to change the conditions of life in modern society in such a way that a growing number of people find it possible to base their political decisions not on specific allegiances, but on complex constellations of interest. This might be the definition of liberalism as the programme of a majority party.

The journey to this destination is longer than the intellectual journey of this brief argument. Liberalism and parties which call themselves liberal are not the same. A programme for a liberal future will not be drafted by party officials; the model of some of the French 'clubs', or of the 'alternative professors' whose report had a major impact on German criminal justice policy, is more likely. That the wind is blowing into the faces of those who engage in this task may in fact help the intellectual freshness of the enterprise; it is much less edifying for life in modern societies that the great conservatism of the social democrats dominates the scene for the time being and that the New Right dominates the opposition. We have got the potential that enables us to combine prosperity and security with a new liberty for many; but we get stuck in the institutions of an economy, polity and society geared to other objectives (and of course in the constitutional lack of imagination of prevailing conditions and of those who like to represent them). For the time being, a new liberalism is the only visible hope for an attempt to tailor reality to fit the potential rather than to cut the potential to fit reality – admittedly an abstract hope which, like German philosophy in Heine's classical analysis of its role, may realize the revolution more radically than actually happened between the conquest of the Bastille and the Thermidor, but which does so only in the mind.

5 The End of the Social-Democratic Consensus?

The Legitimacy of Political Power in Contemporary Societies

It is clearly no accident that right-wing social democrats are the most consistent conservatives in contemporary politics. While so-called conservative parties seek a programmatic basis, including a new morality or even a radical return to yesterday's values, right-wing social democrats manage not only with a minimum of programme, but even with a minimum of government: they do not dispute the prevailing assumptions of economic and social policy, and they devote their time to law and order and to the administration of the *status quo*. I do not propose to take issue with such attitudes just yet; so long as the 'minimal state' does not promise a plausible answer, the reduced state is one possible response to the contradictions of modernity. Nor do I propose to give misplaced concreteness to the substantive discussion by prematurely mentioning names. It is, rather, the intention of this chapter to trace the emergence and significance of a political position which, while it dominates the developed countries of the First World, nevertheless gives the impression of being at the end of its tether, yesterday's world.

How does one become a right-wing social democrat? If one looks at the older exemplars of this species, their careers began with the convinced advocacy of the interests of the under-privileged against the resistance of the privileged; a motive of justice. It found its political expression in a combination of four attitudes which are in fact the essentials not only of the social-democratic consensus, but of modernity itself: in economic policy this attitude never doubts the need for growth by increases of productivity, while gladly accepting the prestabilized harmony between improvements in both the standard of living and the work situation of workers and increases of production. In terms of social policy, the dominant motive is one of equality, usually defined as equality of citizenship rights rather than equality of incomes or general social position, thus as equality of opportunity rather than of results. Politically, these social democrats accept democratic institutions as an instrument of change, indeed, having won at first strong minorities and later majorities by these institutions, they have become their most persuasive advocates. Finally, in the realm of values, and of culture in the widest sense, such social democrats are the main proponents of rationality in the sense of Max Weber, from book-keeping through bureaucracy to science and technology.

Two connected developments of this syndrome of social attitudes are important for the genesis of the right-wing social democrat. One is that their ideas have by and large been realized in the OECD societies. This is a statement which is bound to meet with objections, not least among social democrats. Such objections are clearly not without justification. Equal rights of all citizens in particular – the social element of the consensus – have by no means been fully realized; there are guest workers and immigrants and underpaid woman workers and homosexuals and radicals and others whose social destiny gives no reason for complacency. Nevertheless, it remains true than an extended period of economic growth between the Marshall Plan at the end of the 1940s and the dollar crises at the beginning of the 1970s has brought unheard-of prosperity to many; that citizenship rights in free countries have today been extended from the legal to the political and further to the social sphere; that the institutions of democracy permit the control of power and changes of government; and that science and technology have permeated all parts of life. Thus, the classical social-democratic position has lost its fire. A grand programme has been realized; it is no longer a force for change. One might argue that it is not surprising that those who have advocated this programme and seen it realized during their lifetime now defend the achievements which are written on their banners. Today, the self-satisfied 'You've never had it so good' might well be the election slogan of many right-wing social democrats (although of course it was a social-democratic conservative rather than a conservative social democrat who invented it).

Reference to Harold Macmillan documents the other tendency which I have in mind. To a considerable extent, the ideas which we have sketched had to be implemented against the resistance of ruling classes and parties. They welcomed democracy only as long as it guaranteed their predominance; while the anti-democratic movements of the 1920s were a rearguard action, they betrayed underlying attitudes which were present, if hidden, before. Rationalization and rationality often had to be fought for against the cultural pessimism of a romantic bourgeoisie as well as against the entrepreneurial tyrant. The history of extending citizenship rights is almost identical with the history of the labour movement. Faith in the beauty of economic growth alone was from the beginning a common basis of working class and bourgeoisie; it is apparent here that if one takes a longer view, both stand in fact on the same side, the side of modernity. Both might therefore lose their relevance at the same point of time. But this is not our subject yet. The history of the last one hundred, and above all the last thirty years shows that the resistance of the ruling groups of a century ago has increasingly turned into acceptance of the values of the then opposition. So-called conservative parties have adopted element after element of social-democratic ideas. Thus the hegemony of social-democratic politics began, and it is of no consequences whether it is sustained by a declared Social Democrat like Helmut Schmidt, a declared Liberal like Valéry Giscard d'Estaing, or a declared Conservative like Edward Heath. This is what we call the social-democratic consensus.

Before we take a critical look at this consensus, one remark is in place. It is easy today to pour irony over the political syndrome which marks climax and crisis of modernity; it is all the more important to emphasize that in many respects the social-democratic consensus signifies the greatest progress which history has seen so far. Never before have so many people had so many life chances. Thus the result is well worth defending; and if the social-democratic consensus continues to determine the political scene of the OECD countries for a while, this will produce without doubt more benefits than harm.

Nevertheless, the end of the historical strength of this consensus is in sight. The social-democratic syndrome of values has not only ceased to promote changes and new developments, but it has begun to produce its own contradictions, and it can no longer deal with them effectively. This is the structural background of what one might call the crisis of legitimacy of political power in modern society; there is effective doubt in the adequacy of existing institutions, and of the assumptions on which they are based.

In this analysis, we cannot develop in any detail the figure of theory on which such statements are based; in any case, it is not particularly new or original. It is an attempt to tie the notion of legitimacy as developed in legal and political theory to the structural context of social development. The difficulties of this attempt have been exposed in contemporary social theory above all by the subtle contributions of Jürgen Habermas to our subject. He rejects first of all, with polite determination, all ('empiristic') attempts to regard, following Max Weber, legitimacy as the belief in legitimacy and calls them 'applicable in social science, but unsatisfactory, because they abstract from the systematic value of the reasons of validity'.[1] While this is a criticism of vulgar Weberians rather than of Weber himself, it remains justified. Legitimacy is neither merely what opinion research has to say about sympathies for government or even the constitution, nor is it simply the same as effectiveness of power. Habermas then proceeds to take issue with the 'normativistic' attempt to find pervasive bases of valuation for assessing the justice of power. It is difficult to contradict him when he says that while such an attempt may be satisfactory with respect to the systematic value of the reasons of validity, it remains 'untenable because of the metaphysical context in which it is embedded.[2]

The question which remains wide open, however, is: If we assume that we want to apply the moral yardstick of certain fundamental human rights to all forms of power and government, to Hitler, Stalin, Amin and Pinochet as to the governments which are responsible for Northern Ireland, the Southern United States and German 'guest workers', and if we assume further that we do not want to call any government legitimate which violates these rights – where do we find the reasons for such an attitude? Habermas himself seeks what he calls a 'reconstructive' concept of legitimacy, or rather, of 'legitimation', and he has to introduce three equally difficult notions for the purpose: the 'general interest' to which actions which need legitimation are related; a consistent connection with a 'system of justification' for this interest; and a procedure for judging the rightness or justice of such a system. In the last analysis, Habermas finds it difficult to avoid proximity to historicist assumptions: 'Is there an alternative to the historical injustice of general theories on the one hand and the lack of a standard for mere historical understanding on the other? The only promising programme which I can see is a theory which clarifies in structural terms the sequence of different levels of justification which we can observe in history and then reconstructs it as a context with its own logic of development.'[3]

The suspicion of historicism could be avoided, if the last part of this statement was turned the other way round: the sequence of different levels of justification in history observed in history has to be clarified structurally, *without* any attempt to find a logic of development. This would mean that while we assume that it is possible to distinguish between historical themes – a certain light in which periods of historical development are cast, indeed certain principles, the hegemony of which characterizes such periods – and while we define legitimacy by the factual validity of these principles, we do not assume that there is a 'logical' sequence of hegemonial principles which can be presented as systematic in any sense. In this way it would become possible to describe historical processes of social change without inventing The Path of history (which must surely remain on that rubbish heap of ideas on which Popper has effectively dumped it). Following this approach, the problem of legitimacy in modern societies is serious, because it augurs the end of the effectiveness of a great theme of history, the theme of modernity.

Before we take this idea one or two steps further, we have to admit, however, that it does not help us solve the normative problem of legitimacy, the problem of human rights. Here, I cannot see any answer other than operating with a double concept of legitimacy. There are certain fundamental principles of the political community – articles of the peace treaty on which society is founded in the sense of Hobbes – which accompany the historical process in principle as invariants. Their claim is absolute, whereas other values, such as those of modernity, may determine long periods, but ultimately remain relative. This is the application of the necessary distinction petween invariable elements of the social contract and variable structures of historical societies to the problem of legitimacy.

The variability of structures can be described in the categories of social science. For understanding legitimacy, the relationship between social institutions and social forces is crucial. From one point of view, social institutions as the reality of hegemonial values are always a response to social forces, that is, to the potential of human life chances provided by the economic, social and technical resources of a society. Institutions may be an adequate, in formal terms a flexible, open response to these forces; if and as long as this is the case, there are not likely to be doubts in legitimacy to any considerable extent. It is, however, conceivable – and indeed at times inevitable – that the potential of a society outgrows its reality. Institutions harden and do not bend to the pressures of a new potential. An impression is spreading that there is much that might happen, but does not happen, because one finds oneself in a cage of bondage. These are times in which the representatives of institutions – the ruling class perhaps – find themselves under pressure; doubt in the legitimacy of their power is growing; they encounter (to quote Habermas yet again) first the need of legitimacy and then a crisis of legitimacy.

Here, we are concerned with the question of whether the OECD societies are today in a condition of this kind. It is our thesis that there are indeed signs that the legitimacy needs of the representatives of the social-democratic consensus are growing, although it would not be justified to speak of a crisis of legitimacy. There is, however, much to be said for adding a 'yet' to this statement: it is not yet justified to speak of a crisis of legitimacy; but there are features in the structures of advanced societies which suggest the conclusion that such a crisis may be inevitable.

If one asks today where criticism of the social-democratic consensus comes from, one encounters three important forces. If one wants to give them topical names, one might call them the trend reversers, the system haters, and the ecologists – that is, those who want to turn back the wheel of history; those who want to abolish (or see abolished) existing institutions with no concern about the price or indeed the future; and those who are dreaming of a different world, a different quality.

We have not yet discussed the contradictions of modernity; otherwise it would be clear that there are reasons for all three of these attitudes. This is true even for the strictly reactionary attitude in response to such contradictions. Here, we must confine ourselves to a few references. Modern societies have to a considerable extent become what Margaret Thatcher calls 'pocket-money societies', that is arrangements by which a paternalistic state prescribes very largely what the money of individuals must be spent on, and their remaining income is little more than pocket money. The demand that in a highly developed society the individual himself should carry responsibility for his affairs, including medical care, old-age pensions, schools for the children and housing, becomes understandable before this background. Politically, this position includes not only insistence on more effective measures for maintaining law and order, but also Sam Huntington's answers to the questions of governability;[5] what is needed according to this position is not to 'dare more democracy', but to re-establish lost authority, in the state, in organizations, in the family. What I have called earlier the 'new morality', that is the mystification of the quest for political power by vague talk about the meaning of life, is a part of the same position. We are not interested in cheap criticism here; but the question must at least be raised whether a position of this kind, if it had any chance of realization at all, would not be bound to reproduce along with the old structures the old contradictions and conflicts as well. In any case, the reactionary position is a strategy of confrontation.

This is not as true of the system haters as might appear at first sight. Rejection of 'the system' is a political position which in some countries is both aggravated and obscured by the phenomenon of terrorism. We shall not suggest yet another metaphysics of terrorism here. In any case, it seems at least as important to explain reactions to terrorism as the acts of violence themselves. Why do two dozen incidents upset the whole society of the Federal Republic of Germany, whereas a hundred times that number has not removed entirely a healthy sense of normalcy from Northern Ireland? The German reaction is particularly worrying. What has happened here is that the general – social-democratic – consensus has been narrowed further into a 'minimal consensus' about an in itself narrow interpretation of the constitution, and has at the same time been made unbearably explicit by courts as well as governments. As a result, a lowly official can investigate the 'loyalty to the constitution' of a future city planning officer, postman or engine driver – and a considerable portion of a young generation is deliberately defined out of the official society. Even where there has not been such an explosive narrowness and explicitness of the prevailing consensus, however, fundamental doubts in 'the system' of modern society and its government are widespread. Sometimes one gets the impression that the mild unrest of 1968 has left many with the idea that while economy and state do not deserve their confidence, the same is true also for the more or less patent solutions offered at the time by the left. And many respond to this experience by opting out, by a kind of inner emigration which can take place in communes and sects as well as in drug addiction and ultra-permissiveness. Sometimes, such feelings become virulent, and people want to show the establishment of the social-democratic consensus how little they think of it; perhaps the Liberal vote in Britain in 1974 can be explained at least partly in this way. It is not very far from such situational expressions of frustration to the classical *acte gratuite* of the existentialists, that is, acts which while without meaning confirm one's existence, if only because they annoy others. At the time of the social-democratic consensus, changes of government usually do not lead to any great changes of policy; the consensus weighs on citizens and evokes with some a more or less irrational potential of resistance. This is why the system haters must not be underestimated; their explosive potential in modern societies is considerable, although their ability to shape the future is minimal.

This is the main difference between the system haters and the ecologists, to which other political activists for a better world might be added. While their basic motive may not be dissimilar from that of the system haters, they are at least trying to define the theme of another society. Ideas of this kind have by now a history which is as rich as it is confused: Herbert Marcuse figures in it as does the Club of Rome, Fritz Schumacher and 'The Great Book of Country Living'. If one looks at these positions more closely, they soon reveal their contradictions. Opponents of nuclear power stations usually do not want to forego increasing energy consumption, and the alleged simplicity of country life is in the end the highest, and usually also the most expensive, luxury of the affluent society. Nevertheless, there is – however inarticulate, confused and imprecise it may be – a force in the demand for a new quality of life which the administrators of the social-democratic consensus fear for good reasons. This force cannot only cost the consensus parties votes, but it aims at their very core, at the assumptions on which the consensus is based. It is about changing the subject and the quest for something new – small wonder that government and opposition, trades unions and employers are united in condemning it!

How important are the three forces of doubt in the social-democratic consensus, if one takes them together? The word 'important' conceals several criteria. Still, we are well advised to assume that these forces do not constitute a revolutionary potential, and that their essential significance is at the moment their nuisance value rather than their genuine political weight. There may be elections which are indirectly decided by ten per cent or even twenty per cent voting for a protest party; but the new parties do not survive as such. Moreover, there has always been a degree of unease and dissatisfaction with political institutions; those in government have always been charged with playing things close to their chests; even violence has never been absent from politics for very long. Thus there can be no question of a direct threat to the social-democratic consensus at this time.

In a slightly longer perspective, however, say that of a decade or so, the parties of the consensus will not ignore the messengers of change except at their peril. What is asked from them is no less than a change of approach both in substantive and in formal respects. The consensus parties have grown up with the figure of thought of the class struggle. In their view of history, there is somewhere at the beginning, in the nineteenth century, the classical conflict of bourgeoisie and proletariat. Then, in a second stage – either 1914, or for some late-comers in the 1960s – the festival of reconciliation between the classes took place and the union of working class and bourgeoisie in the form of the new middle class was created. Since then, on a third stage, there are no longer any classes, there are only affluent citizens. In fact, of course, developments were much more complicated. If one works on the assumption that the classical class struggle actually happened (in fact, differences between societies were great at all times), two changes have to be considered above all others. One might be called the fragmentation of class-relevant social positions. While the nineteenth-century industrial worker was a subject in almost every respect, there are many today who have differential chances of access to different institutions. People who are by and large satisfied with their economic condition may nevertheless feel that they are excluded from the quality of a healthy, natural life; there may be a potential for ecologists here. People who can afford to make the contradiction between promise and reality of participation in democratic communities their main concern will either become active in political parties or turn into fundamental critics of the party system. The other development is the enormous extension of chances of mobility. Many people are no longer nailed to their class position. Frequently, there are personal ways out of the social dilemma and towards the realization of interests, without any collective action.

The immediate conclusion from such developments is that the class struggle has lost in intensity by mobility and in formative power for total societies by fragmentation. But this is only a part of the truth. The same set of facts suggests another conclusion as well. In view of fragmentation and mobility the class conflict assumes a situational character. In certain situations – if one lives near Seveso or Windscale, for example, or if one is confronted with evident corruption at the top, or if one temporarily belongs to the educational 'class' – conflict erupts in a widely visible form. At such times its intensity is no less than that of classical conflicts. Persons are removed from office, decisions already taken are reversed. It does not much help those responsible for decisions that the situation passes and that the driving forces do not remain. In this way, an almost *pointilliste* picture of social processes emerges, a nervous jumping from situation to situation. Modern politics has become episodic politics.

It is hard to tell whether a condition of this kind can last or not. The word 'transition' has been abused so much that I prefer to avoid it. A certain instability, however, is unmistakable, if one has on the one hand a broad social-democratic consensus, while on the other hand ever new pin pricks of situational protest punch holes into the silk cushion of the consensus. The condition is further complicated by the fact that the same people sustain the consensus in some respects, but attack it in others. The same civil servant who does not want either his security or his standard of living threatened affords the luxury of demonstrating against nuclear waste disposal in his vicinity;

to say nothing about the paradoxes in the attitudes of some teachers. It is actually striking, and perhaps interesting in terms of social psychology, how relatively easy people seem to find it to live with such contradictions instead of being ground to pieces by them. An older electoral sociology still worked on the assumption that cross-pressures neuroticize people and make them abstain; today, complicated incompatibilities in people's attitudes do not seem to have this effect. It is in fact government which finds it difficult to allow its citizens such incompatibilities; a policeman may not attend a protest meeting against certain government policies. This is how one conducts the class struggle from above.

Legitimation in the sense in which we have used the word here is the process of justifying power in line with the relations of social institutions and forces as well as social classes. Thus power is not legitimated merely by reference to abstract norms, but also by reference to what is and what can be done. Legitimacy is given if and when the credibility of justification is sustained by social institutions which absorb and transform the forces which carry them along. In this sense, legitimacy is always precarious. Institutions have an almost primeval tendency towards ossification, while social forces cannot easily be domesticated.

It can nevertheless be argued that the needs of legitimation of the First World are more than merely inevitable corollaries of the conflictuality of society. (We are not concerned here with societies of the other worlds, though their legitimation needs are if anything greater.) If one tries to find a thread that ties the episodes of contemporary politics together, the one that emerges is that of a used-up subject of history, which may still be defended by the consensus parties for some time and with impressive effort, but which increasingly slips away, whether as an avalanche or by more gradual shifts, and makes room for another, new theme. Today, we can grasp the contradictions of modernity with our hands. All over they transcend the limitations of existing institutions. At the same time, the representatives of these institutions, those in power, are constitutionally unable to master the problems which result from their own assumptions.

Economic growth is one of these basic assumptions. Today it appears as if from a certain point onwards the happy spiral 'technical progress–replacement of human labour–creation of new possibilities of work–further technical progress etc.' no longer works. The work society runs out of work (to use Hannah Arendt's term).⁶ What now? The consensus parties have one prescription only, that is more economic growth. Or: The realization of social citizenship rights requires all kinds of measures of social policy. One needs insurance systems for pensions, a National Health Service, a regional fund and similar institutions. These have to be financed, so that one needs higher taxes. And promptly developments which were meant to be a condition of enfranchisement turn into a new disenfranchisement. People are put on the impersonal leash of giant bureaucracies and at the same time robbed of their freedom of decision by high taxes. But all prescriptions merely aggravate this tendency. Or: Equal opportunities of education are a basic right of modern society. In order to establish them, comprehensive schools are created. But these mean that the very opportunities of differentiation are destroyed which were supposed to be opened to all. The Hirsch paradox in fact aggravates the impression that equality has something like a built-in frustration effect: we pretend to be concerned only with 'material goods' which can be distributed, without noticing that we are in fact dealing with 'positional goods' which are either incapable of distribution (like, say, the position of Pope) or lose their value by generalization (like the solitary hut on a mountain lake).⁷ Or: The opening-up of new life chances for all requires the removal of traditional barriers. Mobility, for example, is possible only if allegiances of family, occupation, place of residence are no longer ascribed, but become to some extent arbitrary. The arbitrariness of linkages, however, can reach a point at which every social movement becomes almost random because there are no co-ordinates within which it can be placed. As a result, people lose their social identity; they find themselves in conditions of life in which meaningless acts become almost an existential necessity. The social contract itself begins to crumble. Such examples could easily be multiplied. The two fashionable subjects of the governability of democracies and the moral ambiguity of science have not even been mentioned yet. They all expose the same pattern: progress creates new problems which cannot be solved with the old tools; but as yet there are no new tools at our disposal to solve them.

This is meant quite specifically. When leading politicians meet today – and this is presumably true even for summit conferences – there is usually one among them who explains at great length that the Phillips curve is no longer a correct description, that floating currencies have not had the expected effect, that free trade does not lead to international justice, and that in any case Keynesian economic tools have lost their grip. The others would then nod in agreement; they share these impressions. But after a short and respectful silence someone will suggest that the Federal Republic of Germany must after all stimulate demand a little more, and Britain must put a stop to its protectionist measures, and the French franc must no longer float as 'dirtily' as it does. This is what I mean if I speak of legitimacy needs: everybody knows that things cannot go on in the same way, but those who carry responsibility cannot think of solutions other than those of yesterday.

Is there a specifically liberal response to the contemporary condition thus described? There certainly is in an abstract sense. The liberal is always concerned about the individual, his life chances, and the reduction to a minimum of all constraints, which restrict its unfolding. The liberal will always resist the greater glory of class, nation, church, or any other collective entity. The liberal is secondly concerned about extending the horizon of human life chances, about exploring new possibilities; he is in that sense the restless element of society. Liberals do not primarily represent social institutions, but they speak in the name of the forces which keep these institutions on their toes and ready to move forward.

It is easy to see that this is not a description of political

E

parties which call themselves liberal. Most liberal parties have today become a part of what we have called the social-democratic consensus. They may defend its positions a little more amusingly than others and give them a little colour; but as a rule their imagination is no less limited than that of the former left and the former right. Indeed, who is to take issue on that with the parties which represent a consensus which is after all very successful? I hope that these deliberations have left no doubt that I do not want to criticize modernity, but I want to show that it creates its own problems and in that sense encounters boundaries which are beyond guilt and repentance.

If one is not prepared to accept the episodic politics of which we have spoken, one has, in the present condition, little to do and much to think about. At a time at which the great consensus in its boredom represses its legitimacy needs, it is above all important to understand what is happening. If such understanding succeeds, it might well become a force of change itself. In a sense, the right-wing social democrats who administer power are sad creatures, because it is so obvious that they represent yesterday's world. But in saying this, one has to remember that for the time being they are not doing any great harm. In a sense, there is no better condition than to be administered by them. Certainly, our affairs would be in worse hands with reactionaries, system haters and even ecologists. However, this makes the impatient quest for understanding and for designs of the future the most important liberal task.

The question remains how the process will continue which we have described here primarily from its negative side of the dissolution of the prevailing consensus. The analyst is well advised to approach this question with caution. The themes of history are not connected either by a straight line or by a dialectical pattern or by any other rigid logic of development. There may be progress and regress, and above all totally unexpected and different things. Thus one might suspect that it is unlikely that the answer to the new problems will be more government. One may assume that the structures of the work society, centred as it is around jobs and labour, will not suffice for tomorrow. One may hope that the social construction of human lives will give room to qualities which the expansion-oriented society has neglected. One may even consider that a new social contract should or could be concluded in which law and order are not primarily guaranteed by a bigger police force or harsher punishments. But it is quite conceivable that real developments will take an entirely different turn.

6 Inequality, Hope and Progress

The purpose of the deliberations of this chapter may seem outrageous, but it defies simple categories. It has to do with hope, the principle of which the Marxian philosopher Ernst Bloch rightly says that it above all moves men to improve their conditions and ultimately their lives. But it also has to do with reality, thus with hope not as opium for the people but as wholesome food here and now. Since it is the desire for real improvements of the human condition which moves me to argue the case for inequality – or should I have said for liberty? – it may even be that some may feel stimulated to reconsider their own entrenched values. For what I want to develop is an exercise in anti-cyclical thinking, necessary perhaps, but hardly pleasing.

Modern societies are based on the principle of giving as many people as much as possible. There are several ways of formulating this principle – the utilitarian way of 'the greatest happiness of the greatest number', the Marxian way 'to each according to his need, from each according to his ability', or more generally as 'the full development of the capacities of all' – but in one way or another the twin assumptions, that society should enhance the life chances of its members and that everybody's life chances are equally important, are built into constitutions, party manifestos, and the invisible ideological baggage of most of us. In the last two centuries, the notion that anybody's life chances are as important as those of everybody else has proved a strong force of social dynamics, sometimes of revolution. But few of those who promoted the idea regarded it as a purpose in itself. Equality seemed desirable because men are different, and in order to enable people to be different in their own right rather than at the expense, or at the mercy, of others. The purpose of equality is inequality, the purpose of general rights is different individual lives.

But revolutions involve their own alienation; before they have completed their course it becomes difficult to disentangle means and ends. The harder it is to create the alleged preconditions, that is, equality, the more remote becomes the purpose for which they are created, that is, liberty. In our case, the paradox of alienation is even more dramatic. To the extent to which equality has come to occupy the actions of those who make decisions as well as the minds of those who think about them, we have lost sight of the differences which alone give the greatest life chances to the greatest number; and to the extent to which political thought and action have thus been foreshortened, society itself has become rigidly unable to effect the changes necessary in order to create the colourful world in which a hundred flowers bloom on the same fertile soil. For a society in which all are equal in all respects is also one devoid of realistic hope and thus of incentives for progress.

There are obvious questions about this kind of argument. Is it not a familiar conservative defence of privilege? To argue that inequality produces hope and hope is the stimulus of progress can certainly be construed to mean that the man in the dole queue should be pleased about the tycoon who flies to Monte Carlo in his private plane in order to gamble away the lifetime earnings of a workman in a single weekend. Or is the case progressive after all, if in a slightly unfamiliar vein? To argue that equality is not the end, but merely the beginning of progress, and that such progress must be stimulated by hope which in turn presupposes difference must surely worry the defenders of that new civilization in which everybody is equally poor, and emigration is regarded as the only escape from the condition of oppressive drabness and drab oppression. This ambivalence of the argument is an important complication which we shall keep in mind, though I shall hardly begin to resolve it.

Then there is the other set of questions, the meaning of the terms, inequality, hope, progress. Take 'inequality': has not Christopher Jencks shown that we cannot have equality even if we want it, and John Rawls that equity, or fairness, is what we should aim for?[1] Or 'hope': 'Reason cannot blossom without hope, hope cannot speak without reason,' says Ernst Bloch.[2] But does he mean hope for the totally different, Utopia, or hope for what can actually be achieved? Then 'progress': Tawney was the last person whom I heard speak about progress without an apparent sense of embarrassment; and Morris Ginsberg was surely right when he said: 'The idea of progress which dominated all thought in the latter part of the nineteenth century began to be seriously questioned in the beginning of this century, and in the interval between the wars there was a widespread impression that it was about to be relegated to the realm of exploded myths.'[3]

Ginsberg had courage; he revived the old idea in 1944 when surely the signs were for frightening regression rather than progress, at least in the moral terms which interested him. Yet he may well have been right, at least in a longer perspective. The abandonment of Plato's idea that some are born with gold and others with iron, or of Aristotle's notion that some are by nature privileged to live the theoretical life of leisure whereas others cannot but live the practical life of work – ideas which had dominated the centuries despite the apparent, if deceptive, egalitarianism of Christian faith – marks a great step forward by all accounts. When at last it became accepted that every man and woman has the same right to unfold his or her faculties and be creative, and that it is for the community to create the preconditions of the exercise of this right, modern society began, and with it unheard-of chances for unheard-of numbers of people. In this sense, equality has meant, and continues to mean, moral progress.

Leaving terminological niceties aside, such equality has involved, in terms of practical change, two processes: the progressive extension of citizenship rights, and the effective domestication of power. How citizenship has come to acquire an increasingly full meaning has often been described; I still feel that T. H. Marshall's analysis is unrivalled.[4] It began with the rights of man; all men are equal before the law. But equality before the law means little if the power to make law is confined to the few. Thus political equality, the right to form associations, free speech, and universal suffrage came to supplement legal equality. Again, it was soon clear that this would not suffice. If a person cannot get a proper education, indeed if he is dependent for his living on the arbitrary decisions of others, if he is unprotected in illness or old age – what meaning has equality got? Today we know that the process of defining social citizenship rights is open-ended; the right to a minimum wage, to old-age pensions, to health provisions, to a decent home, to education are merely the beginnings of a long and perhaps endless list; but while this fact points to the heart of the problem which I want to discuss here, only the most anachronistic conservative would claim today that there is no such thing as social citizenship rights, and his claim would be quite ineffective.

Domestication of power, the other side of the coin, is the recurrent subject of political theory and analysis from Montesquieu to Max Weber and beyond. Perhaps it would be possible to chart a course of this trend which runs parallel to the extension of citizenship. Certainly, the early methods for limiting the use of power were somewhat formal: the separation of powers, parliaments with limited rights, restrictions on royal prerogative, indeed the idea of a constitution itself. When Weber described the legal or rational legitimation of power (as distinct from that based on tradition or charisma), he thought of more than formal rules of government by generalized norms (and their bureaucratic administration) throughout the political community. Since his time, and to the present day, a wide social aspect of the domestication of power has been uppermost in people's minds: How can one prevent the translation of sectoral power, in industry for example, or the military, or the secret service, into political power? How can the rational legitimation of power be extended to all society? And how can one make sure that an eminent position with respect to social status, an aristocratic name, a very high income, is not abused for the illegitimate exercise of power? Tax legislation, industrial participation and co-determination, Watergate investigations, rules to control multi-national companies, and many other topical issues may be seen in this context.

The rationale of this two-pronged process is both evident and plausible. If all men are to have equal opportunities to develop their talents, interests, even eccentricities and idiosyncracies, there has to be a common floor on which they stand. That floor is provided by citizenship rights, and the higher it is the better. But apart from this positive approach one has to make sure also that nobody is in a position to restrict the life chances of others, or indeed their citizenship rights, arbitrarily. There must not be colonels of mercenary armies, slave-holders, men who can make others squirm or starve, buy their votes or their loyalties, nor must there be uncontrolled influence by Lockheed directors or CIA heads, Teamster bosses or Mafia chiefs. Apart from the common floor, the social fabric has to have a ceiling, although one might argue that this should not be as low as possible, but only as low as necessary.[5]

So far the picture we have drawn is in fact no more than a picture; it is static when it should be a drama, a process. Clearly, neither equal citizenship rights nor the domestication of power have been fully achieved. It would be easy to make an emotional case against persisting inequalities of opportunity on the basis of race, sex, social origin; and the examples quoted show only too clearly how much undomesticated power there is still around. Indeed, it seems likely that both these preconditions of a just society will never be fully achieved, because as we move on, new threats to equal opportunities develop which require new responses by the law, politics, and society. But while this is so, and in a sense by the same token, there are also signs that both processes have in some respects overshot the mark which they were supposed to reach. It could be argued that at times the space between floor and ceiling of the building of modern society has become so squeezed that many are unable to stand upright or, to change the metaphor, that modern citizens have domesticated power and yet they find themselves in that iron cage of bondage of Max Weber's which makes the realization of life chances as impossible as change, and both for the same set of reasons.

First the facts, and let us begin with what happens if citizenship stretches beyond itself, as it were, that is, if equality of opportunity becomes equality of results, and if equal life chances turn into equal lives. This is the trend towards the abolition of inequalities of equal status.

Education is a case in point. When I myself pleaded, a decade ago, for 'education as a civil right', the argument was one which is familiar today.[6] Equality of educational opportunity is a basic right of every citizen, because education is both a prerequisite and a dimension of full social and political participation. Such equality of opportunity is threatened not only by legal obstacles, or by overt social and economic barriers, but by less visible barriers as well. Working-class children grow up at a considerable social distance from institutions of higher learning, a distance of information, a distance of motivation, a distance of culture. It is thus necessary not only to abolish school fees and supply school buses, but also to inform parents and children systematically about opportunities which are available to them, to motivate them for higher education, to enable them to go along this road without having to abandon all the cultural attributes of their social origin. Clearly, citizenship thus conceived extends far beyond even Marshall's notion of its 'social' aspects, and somewhere along this road one crosses the line where the abolition of obstacles – that is, of differences – slides over from the creation of equal opportunities to the creation of equal status. At the end of this road, and by no means in fiction only, equality of educational opportunity is thought of as requiring the replacement of the Queen's English by class dialects, and the rearrangement of curricula so as to enable children of all groups to succeed equally, or at least in proportion to the size of their groups. 'We will,' to quote Christopher Jencks, 'have to change the rules of the game so as to reduce the rewards of competitive success and the costs of failure.'[7] Comprehensive schools are created not to offer a more varied set of opportunities to more children but to organize the quality of all.

Daniel Bell has analyzed this particular aspect of the dynamics of citizenship in the chapter on 'Meritocracy and Equality' in his book *The Coming of Post-Industrial Society*. We owe him many insights. The 'change in social temper' to which he refers is in fact one of those jumps from quantity to quality where a little more citizenship changes the entire complexion of society. In education this means a transition from equality of opportunity to equality of the result of the educational effort. Already, so Bell concludes, 'the concept of equality of result has become the Archimedean point of a major new effort to provide a philosophical foundation – a concept of justice as fairness – for a communal society.'[8]

Nor is this process confined to education. It is difficult to place any other interpretation on the reduction of income differentials than the view that there is no justification for inequalities of income. In some countries, important political groups have stated the limits of justifiable inequality explicitly: nobody should earn more than seven times the average earnings of the lowest paid (says the Trades Union Congress in Britain), or more than DM 12,000 a year (according to the Young Socialists' organization in Germany). Flat-rate increases and progressive taxation accelerate developments in this direction. It is more than a footnote to this analysis that the process of equalization of status has long passed beyond what sociologists call achieved social status towards positions which are ascribed in that they are based on immutable attributes of individuals. Men and women are not merely to be given the suffrage and equal wages for equal work, but they are to be treated as equals in all respects; society is to be arranged in such a way that differences of sex can be ignored. An analogous development has long set in with respect to age, one of the oldest sources of the differential distribution of power.

Citizenship is a set of equal rights, and rights are in one respect chances, opportunities to make choices within given linkages. It is commonplace today that such rights cannot be given by writing them into constitutions and laws. But the process of creating the conditions under which citizenship rights become real has gone far beyond the legal, political, and socioeconomic realms. As social groups and their spokesmen have discovered the intrinsic incompleteness of equal opportunities, and the political payoff of more radical demands, they have turned their attention to inequalities which are at the core of any social structure. The distinction between equal rights and equal status, between a levelling of opportunities for choice and a levelling of the choices themselves, has come to be blurred and eventually abandoned. It may be argued, of course, that the distinction was at all times in part a defence mechanism by the haves against the have-nots. By abandoning it, however, imperceptibly at first, then with growing momentum, the extension of equal rights of citizenship has created a condition under which these rights lose much of their meaning: they offer choices which can no longer be made, they promise differential life chances which no longer exist. If it is true that citizenship presupposes a differentiated structure of linkages to which its rights and opportunities are related, it now appears that the dynamics of citizenship sets in motion a process of fundamental change in social structures by dissolving bonds and linkages and thus in the end denying the citizen the fruit of his labours.

An analogous case can be made for the other aspect of equality in modern societies, the domestication of power. Champions of citizenship have always assumed that the new status provides equal opportunities to choose in a world of unequal options. They underestimated the radicalness of the change which they set in motion by presupposing a structured universe of ligatures or linkages. Today it has become apparent that the new citizen is liable to destroy that universe at the risk of reducing his own field of action. What this means with respect to inequalities of power, or rather, of socially structured positions of authority, is most evident if we look at the story of political participation.

One aspect of the domestication of power is representative government. It provides a framework for the citizen to express his political choices and take part in the life of the republic; it sets up institutions for stimulating and controlling government action; it provides checks and balances for the exercise of power without stifling initiative. Like equality of opportunity for unequal choices, it is characterized by a peculiar balance between sameness and difference. While all have the right to vote, and to be elected, to join political parties and take part in political debate, only a few are in positions, albeit restrained by numerous rules, to exercise the right to enact laws and thus to determine the conditions defining people's status, including possibly the status of citizenship; there are ordinary citizens and representative citizens. Again, in other words, the idea of an equal status of citizenship was associated with the more or less explicit assumption of an unequally structured universe of participation, and again – it appears today – the champions of citizenship underestimated the dynamics of the idea.

For once the citizen was born, he did not rest content with the place he was assigned as a participant in the process of representative government. A limited initial set of participation rights provided a lever for demanding more. Up to a point, this was a demand within an undisputed framework of representative government: the abolition of unequal voting rights, the extension of suffrage, higher voter turnout, the creation of adequate conditions for the organization of political parties of all descriptions. But developments did not stop there: they have led, more recently, to a revival of the demand for participatory democracy which has considerable ramifications of a constitutional and political character. Perhaps this trend is not yet as concentrated and massive as that which leads from equal opportunities to equal results, but some of the markers on the road from equal participation rights to equal participation itself can no longer be overlooked.

Let me again mention a few examples without examining them in any detail. The demand for constitutional elements of direct democracy is growing. In some countries, such as France, it has been institutionalized; in others, such as Britain and Germany, it is used in certain cases. More significant than organized referenda, or the direct election to important offices, is the rapid growth of 'citizens' initiatives' – of more or less *ad hoc* organizations to prevent the construction of a nuclear reactor, demand the abolition of the death penalty (or the reverse), join forces to fight for nursery facilities, etc. The community politics movement is of course part of the same syndrome. In the context of this trend it seems significant that in many countries the representative is increasingly assuming features of the delegate. To begin with, this occurs in a practical manner. Candidates for office are severely cross-examined; between elections, constituency and party meetings become more frequent; articulation of voter interests creates a yardstick for measuring the 'loyalty' of representatives; possibly, the number of cases where representatives are not re-elected is growing. In some places, the trend goes further; in a number of German cities, for example, and in many students' unions, the *imperative Mandat* has become a fact, if one of doubtful constitutional status, at least for office-holders of the left. As those who hold office become delegates, it is understandable that the demand for equal representation (to use the word in a less technical sense) should grow. Groups have to be represented in proportion to their importance in the population, women, people from all regions, members of religious and ethnic groups, and whatever other categories may be relevant. And in order to safeguard the participation of all in everything, delegate government is coupled with organized so-called 'parities' in governing bodies, 'equal' representation of students, junior staff and senior staff on university senates, and 'equal' representation of capital and labour on the boards of industrial enterprises.

If there is an undertone of irony in this description, I hope I am not misunderstood. Participation is a civil right too, and the original notion of citizenship certainly imposed unjustified restrictions on its exercise. Indeed, every one of the measures cited, from community politics to co-determination, from citizens' initiatives to the demand for the representation of hitherto unrepresented groups, has its justice and logic. And yet the dynamics of participation provides another example of how the idea of citizenship has released a development which in the end is liable to defeat its own purpose. As equality, when it spreads from opportunities to results, makes choices impossible, so participation can lead to a *verzuiling* (to use a colourful Dutch expression), a 'pillarization' and cementing of the structures of government which makes it all but meaningless to take part in the process of making decisions.

Take the case of delegation, the mandate given to elected office-holders. It is certainly right in principle that those who hold elective office should recognize – and be committed to representing – the views and interests of their electors; in the past, the principle of representation has at times been grossly abused. But if the demand is pressed to the limit, its result is equally frightening in theory and in practice. In theory it means that the holder of elective office is unable to make any move without the explicit approval of his electors. Such approval is hard to come by; it takes time and, moreover, long, almost interminable discussions. The delegate is unable to react quickly to new situations and problems. He is above all unable to lead, that is, to introduce an innovation before it has been accepted by all; he has neither incentive nor real possibility for being ahead of his electorate. This is bad enough, for it means inaction instead of action, immobility instead of progress. In practice, the situation is even worse, and not uncharacteristic-ally so. For in fact little analysis is needed to show that the representative turned delegate will become the spokesman for a rather small group of citizens: not the entire electorate but a party organization, and not the whole party organization, but only the activists who can afford to meet frequently and for long hours of inconsequential debate.

The point bears generalization. I submit that the permanent participation of all in everything is in fact a definition of total immobility. Instead of the dialectic of initiative and control which guarantees that innovation takes place but is not un-checked, it would mean a mixture of permanent theoretical debate and permanent practical inaction. It is difficult to deny that parts of some European universities have reached this stage of *rigor mortis*, but there are less extreme if equally telling examples. Is it an accident that Switzerland, where a popular majority is required, has introduced women's suffrage later than almost all other countries and only recently rejected, in a plebiscite, the reduction of the voting age to eighteen? Contrary to the beliefs of many, innovation and participation are not natural allies; and an optimal balance between the two requires restrictions on the permanent participation of all in everything: majority voting, for example, or representative government.

This is the theoretical side of things, the case for limits on participation. Here, too, the new citizen is about to over-reach himself, to create conditions which would make the very principle useless which he tries to establish. If the political society is organized in such a way that all groups are represented everywhere, and representatives are in fact delegates, then decisions become virtually impossible, and participation loses all meaning. All that is left is a right to be present at endless debates, but no longer a chance to do things, to effect changes, however modest they, or the contribution of the individual citizen to them, may be. But the practical problem is more difficult still. I did not use the words *rigor mortis* lightly. Even a slowdown of the process of innovation can be deadly in modern societies. Such systematic deceleration of change is in fact almost a definition of a revolutionary situation, or at any rate of one which calls for dramatic change. The temptation is great to analyze Marx's notion of the final communist society, or Rousseau's romantic image of the free consensus of free men, as involuntary descriptions of states in which problems can only be solved by extreme suppression, by tyranny. Nothing calls for *Herrschaft* (authority) as much as the attempted realization of the utopian ideal of *Genossenschaft* (association), and nothing for the disenfranchisement of the citizen as the practice of total participation. This is where phenomena of anomie, that is the dissolution of linkages, and the *verzuiling* of the political process by total participation join hands.

This then is the case as it looks at this point of the argument: The process called equality which spreads effective citizenship rights to all, and domesticates political power, carries within it a strain towards over-reaching its goal. As it turns into a demand for the abolition of inequalities of status as well as power, it begins to defeat its own purpose. It is no longer difficult to extrapolate current trends to a point at which equal opportunities become meaningless because there are no differences left to choose from, and equal rights of participation lose meaning because the individual cannot effect any change. To the practical one might add the aesthetic case. A world of equal status and the participation of all in everything would be a drab place, rather like the visible face of the communist countries of Eastern Europe in terms of status, and the tired boredom of an overdrawn party meeting in the back room of a club after closing hours in terms of power. Why is it that working men and women tend to leave in disgust the meetings of their local party once it has been taken over by teachers and students? Partly because they have to work the next morning, but partly also because they sense the pointlessness of it all. And why is it that so many East Europeans have left the paradise in which their governments say they are living? Because they want to have options, read different newspapers, go to Italy or Lappland for their holidays, give up their job in the country to go to town (or vice versa), make a choice between different political parties. Both the practical and the aesthetic case against equality as it turns from opportunities to actual positions carry weight. Yet neither of them answers as such the question which underlies the argument of this chapter: We have seen that there is justification for extended citizenship rights and the domestication of power, in that sense for equality. Is there any justification for inequality? If so, what kind of inequality can be justified? What practical consequences flow from the theoretical case? We have, I believe, assembled the elements of an answer to this question; what remains is to put them together.

Whether human societies always progress in moral as well as technical terms is more than only doubtful. Our own century has not only seen technical and moral progress fall apart, but it has also seen unforgettable examples of moral regression. That there is a case for moral progress seems to me much less doubtful; the imperfections of human society are painfully obvious at a time which seems to have come full circle from the precarious existence of primitive life through modernity and civilization to new threats to the survival of the human race. That it would be dangerous to foreclose the possibility of progress is so plausible as to seem almost beyond dispute. We are living in a world of uncertainty, in which nobody knows all the answers, and those who claim that they do cannot prove that their answers are right. Under such conditions, it is all-important to preserve the possibility of change, to keep societies open. The possibility of progress, however, implies the necessity of social and political change.

But how does change come about? At several points in this volume we have discussed the instruments which might enable one to discover the 'law of development' of capitalist, or any other societies. We have also spoken of the extreme case of revolution. A revolutionary situation is one in which an organized suppressed class stakes its claim in terms of a new set of forces of production. Or again, a revolutionary situation is one in which a common condition of deprivation on the part of one group is accompanied by mismanagement and growing self-doubt on the part of the other, with an internal or external crisis adding to the predicament. But neither explanation suffices as such; and indeed, Marx was almost certainly wrong when he claimed, with a Hegelian figure of thought, that the moment of greatest need (on the part of the proletariat) was also the moment of greatest necessity (of the communist revolution). Extreme deprivation produces lethargy rather than a fighting spirit. The spark which is needed in order to turn a revolutionary situation into a revolution is hope, in the general sense hope of success of course, and more specifically signs that opportunities are real, the sudden admission of a hitherto banned organization, a surprising increase in wages or decrease in taxes, or the like. And it may well be argued that the spark which sets fire to a revolutionary situation is only an extreme case of a more general force which operates in social changes of a gradual character as well. It is the vision of the different, of new and improved life chances, which turns resentment, or any kind of latent desire, into action and thus into change. Whoever has given up hope has in fact accepted the conditions around him; in this sense there is no change without hope.

But hope can mean at least two things, and both have played a part in the social changes of modernity. Hope can be the attraction of a vision of the world that is totally different from all known experience, the inverse of the facts of life: immortality, eternal happiness, universal goodness, and above all, certainty. Faith, love and hope may be sentiments of this world, but they are often motivated by the charms of another, entirely different, world. It has been said that revolutionary ideologies have a religious quality, and to the extent that both promise certainty and fulfilment this is true. But the transcendental vision of revolutions is at least claimed to be of this world: the individual who feels at home again as a fish in the water, human beings who can see and hear and feel for the first time (to use the words of the young Marx in his *Paris Manuscripts*). Since then many versions of such hope have been formulated, generally in the form of some kind of altruistic anarchy in which multi-dimensional men create and unfold their ligatures freely. Such utopian hope can be a powerful motive of change; but it does not promote any specific, identifiable change. Instead, it is both expression and stimulus of a revolutionary situation: if it spreads, this tells a story about social conditions, and it adds sweeping demands for change to them. But they are demands for that wholesale change which in fact provides some with new positions of influence and most with little improvement of their chances of life. Revolutions happen when all other avenues of change are blocked, and the same is true of the spread of utopian hope; it is incapacity to cope with the years ahead which leads to millenial solutions. But they do not solve anything, for such hope is invariably disappointed; revolutionary dreams never come true, and whether religious dreams do, we shall probably never know. Such figments of the imagination are in any case not what is meant here by the link between hope and progress.

For there is another kind of hope which is based on experience, however vicarious this may be: the villa one has seen on a Sunday morning walk, the television film about the games of the rich in Monte Carlo, the description of an exemplary life. Hope in this sense is not about the ultimate stretch of the human imagination, but about the visible potential of human life chances, about things which can happen, because they do happen. This is an important point which cannot be repeated too often: the best proof of possibility will forever be reality. Such hope motivates people to change their conditions, or their lives, in a variety of ways. It may be a stimulus for the individual to move, either geographically, or in the scales of social status. It may be a challenge for solidarity action, in associations, trade unions or political groups, in order to gain (say) shorter working hours for all members. It may be international action, the demand for more voting rights in the International Monetary Fund, or membership in the OECD. And in all cases such hope is coupled with demands for change which are capable of implementation, specific demands for promotion or a salary increase, the forty-eight hour or forty-hour week, new uses for special drawing rights, and the like. Whether every change brought about under social conditions in which action is sparked off by realistic hope is also progress may be open to doubt; but if there is to be any progress at all, such hope is one of its ingredients.

Hope itself, in order to be realistic, must be based on the reality of the conditions hoped for. It is based on the knowledge that some individuals, groups or countries possess what others aspire to. This need not be inequality in rank; the family which spent its holidays in Spain this year and wants to go to Greece next year is motivated by hope as is the working man who moves from West Virginia to California. But often it is status inequality that makes for hope, the desire to improve one's conditions in order to reach a status comparable to that of neighbours, bosses, or others known by more indirect ways. The very least that can be said is that existing inequalities add an element of reality to hope and thus give substance to the demand for change; it may well be that without this admixture hope would not be relevant for change, and thus for progress at all.

I shall stop the theoretical analysis at this point, speculative and open-ended as it is bound to remain. What, for example, can be thought of as a legitimate basis of inequality: educational achievement only, or other criteria as well? Or, as a more narrowly theoretical issue: If real inequalities give rise to effective hope and motivate change, how do these inequalities themselves come about? Must one not assume some kind of qualitative jump somewhere which does not itself arise from the desire to spread existing chances of life? One probably must, and in the following chapter we shall explore some of the conditions under which such mutations take place. But here I want to return briefly to the body of this analysis: What lines of orientation and of action seem plausible, if progress depends on hope and this in turn on inequality? What, in other words, follows from the case made here for the theory of political action if we assume that keeping the door to progress open is in itself a necessary, although not a sufficient, condition of progress?

Our analysis of the social and the political dimensions of equality suggests two answers, and they help to clarify what is meant by inequality in this context. The first answer relates to status, that is, to inequalities of income, of prestige, of position, and of real life chances generally. If it is true that the strain towards equality inherent in modern societies has reached the point at which restrictions on the range of available choices make nonsense of the opportunities opened up by citizenship – and there are those who would doubt this assertion – then it would follow that an acceptable balance requires concentration on a new theme. We have described this theme in a variety of ways; in any case, it has something to do with ligatures, or linkages. But one element of such linkages consists of tolerable, even desirable inequality. (One may wonder whether ligatures always imply inequalities.) This should clearly not detract from a full status of citizenship for all, nor should it reinstate a kind of domination that enables some to restrict arbitrarily the life chances of others; it is unlikely that such reversals would be tolerable in any modern society anyway. But since human politics is (fortunately) not of the Platonic kind, advancing straight to the perfect solution with the help of philosopher-kings, but proceeds in a more dialectical fashion, there may well be a case for an inequality party: promoting differentiation rather than integration in education, tax relief rather than further relief of income differentials, encouragement for success in industry rather than subsidies for those in trouble, incentives for individual mobility, geographical and otherwise, because this serves to uphold a sense of hope and thus possible progress. Nor are acceptable inequalities confined to the world of the protestant ethic; they are just as significant in an improving society in which people enhance their life chances by moving laterally (as one would say today), in and out of education and jobs for instance, with their ability to control time as the main dimension of difference.

The other answer relates to the structure of government, both public and private. The international debate about the governability of democracies has brought up, in the last few years, a rather disturbing new demand for authority, even for authoritarian rule. Problems have become so complex (or so some say, including conservatives like S. Huntington as well as social democrats like R. Heilbroner),[9] and the threats to survival so imminent, that we have to stop the erosion of governmental responsibility and reinstate powerful authorities operating without an accountability which is bordering on exposure. Such nostalgia, if realized, would lead us to re-enact the last half-century all over again and fight the old battles a second time, quite apart from the human cost involved in turning back the wheels of history. But there is a case for emphasizing the need for initiative in the government of all social institutions, and to encourage initiative as well as responsibility. I have always regarded the American constitution as one of the great inventions of human history; and one, above all, which is practicable, as the last two hundred years have shown. It is not immune to abuse, but capable of self-correction, and above all it institutionalizes, by the dynamic balance between president and congress, both initiative and control in a manner from which many institutions elsewhere could profit. Wherever feasible, a strong case could be made for the separate legitimation of those who take the lead, literally and metaphorically speaking, and those who make sure that people are not misled beyond the inevitable. This is a plea against government by committee, let alone by mandate and permanent debate, although it is also a plea for effective checks and balances conceived as such and encouraged in their operation.

It is the desire for real improvement of the human condition which moves me to argue the case for inequality – so I said in introducing this chapter, and added for good reason: 'or should I have said, for liberty?' Liberty, more liberty that is, at all times requires progress; it is motive and substance of change for the better. Progress at all times requires hope, realistic hope in the possibility of improvement. In order to be realistic, hope has to be based on evidence, on real conditions. We have passed through a phase in which the most powerful hopes of men in advanced societies were inspired by 'democracy in America', as Tocqueville grudgingly praised it, that is, by equality. What I am trying to suggest, with all due caution and many reservations which I hope have become clear in the course of this argument, is that the time has come to look for inspiration in different values, perhaps something like 'opportunity and initiative in America', or anywhere else for that matter. Today hope springs from difference rather than sameness, and liberty from inequality rather than equality.

7 Representative Activities

We are living in an imperfect world. Human beings are ἐνδεές, in need of things. Human needs are capable of growing, as are human faculties to satisfy them. In terms of life chances, this process may mean progress, through we do not know where, indeed whether, it ends. (We are living in a condition of uncertainty.) The mechanism of progress is conflict. From time to time it produces new things, new ways of satisfying needs. The word 'produce' is unduly precise. New ways are not produced as a steel rod is produced in a rolling mill. Being mutations, new ways emerge. We can specify some of the conditions which make emergence possible, even probable. If we are optimistic, we assume that mankind always solves the problems which it faces; if we are not, we can argue that mankind sometimes, or often, misses its chance. But where do the ideas come from which make the emergence of new ways possible?

Why ideas? There is an enormous and all but useless literature about the role of ideas. Vulgar Marxists seem to imply that ideas are 'generated' by or 'derived' from 'real conditions'. That is obscure metaphorical language. The *Critique of Pure Reason* does not emerge by squeezing Prussian society. Vulgar idealists claim that ideas make history. That again is obscure metaphorical language. Weapons do not win wars; they have to be used by someone, and used effectively. Using them is not necessarily a conscious process; it is like speaking prose all one's life. Nobody suggests that the first capitalist 'applied' the protestant ethic.

The figure of analysis, then, is clear and simple. (Gramsci, without undue subtlety, has seen it.) There is a reservoir of ideas at any time. It includes many 'relevant' and 'non-relevant' items. Social groups, or individuals, borrow from this reservoir, and thereby define relevance. Ideas become the aura, and substance, of the exercise of power. Thus there is the *hegemony* of ideas, their validity. By this, ideas become official, with sanctions attached to them, an order of merit for those who propound them, no promotion to senior lecturer for those who do not. There are also relevant opposition ideas, -a rather than non-a, likewise picked out for their usefulness. Those who propound them may not be promoted, but they are applauded by the many. The interplay of ideas and actions offers wide scope for analysis; but the question of the primacy of one or the other is quite pointless. Action without ideas is meaningless; ideas without action are irrelevant.

What ideas? This sounds as if ideas are political programmes. The sound is misleading, indeed wrong. By ideas I mean all products of the human mind. (Here it would be tempting to continue: . . . which are x, y, z . . . and state a number of restrictions, such as: which are original, have found a lasting form, etc.) Moreover, there is not just the world of overall socio-political action to which they relate. Certain areas of human activity have evolved their own action patterns: the world of science, or of painting. There is, in other words, such a thing as sectoral hegemony, of relativity theory, of impressionist style. The world of ideas is a huge and in principle chaotic reservoir of possible relevance, from which given structures of power pick out elements for validation.

If ideas are a necessary condition of emergence and progress, the question remains: Where do they come from? The precise meaning of this question is not easy to ascertain. Nor it is easy to decide whether the question is important. Unless one assumes – we do not – that ideas emerge when they are needed ('where there's a problem, there's a solution'), the field of explanation is wide open. Ideas can emerge anywhere, anytime, and it does not really matter where and when. This will not satisfy the historian/sociologist of ideas, of course; but theories of serendipity emphasize the mystery of the emergence of ideas. We will not pursue this here.

But there is one question which we have to pursue. The carriers of ideas, including new ideas, are people. We may not know, in the sense of being able to predict, who will have an idea when and how (although we know it in retrospect). It may be easier to tell under which conditions it is unlikely that anyone will have an idea, that is, there are conditions which are unfavourable to creativity. If scientists get no money for experimentation; if the publication of unwelcome ideas is outlawed; if a society gets so self-satisfied that no one is listening; etc., etc.; then ideas are unlikely to come forward. (An important difference to consider, though, is: whether ideas are not generated at all, or whether they merely fail to see the light of day. The effect on action may be the same, but for understanding the history of ideas the difference is important.) However these conditions may look, one point remains: there are obviously some people who have – who produce, generate, express – ideas in the sense in which we have used the word. Who are they? What is their specific role? What is their place in society? What does it mean for the human condition that there are such people?

In these brief and deliberately dogmatic remarks I have cut through an enormous tangle of literature under the heading of 'ideology'. This seems to intrigue social scientists as much as any subject, and yet much that is said here is strangely barren. I have no intention of reviewing this literature here; but there may be a case for setting out briefly the kinds of problems which it is intended to deal with, that is, to raise questions.

One starting point of the literature on ideology is the discovery that it is not enough to have an idea. Ideas have an effect only under certain conditions. They may be a necessary condition of effectiveness, but the sufficient condition is the state of social affairs. Do men make history? Yes, but (no but) conditions have to be ripe and ideas have to be there for something to happen. One of Marx's points was to remind people of this connection. Weber's *Protestant Ethic* with its methodological caution and analytical subtlety is a splendid illustration of the point.

The other starting point of the literature is related to the first, although it turns it round, as it were. Ideas have to be used to become effective – that means also that ideas are used. Ideas, and those who produce them, can become the slaves of interests. People can be bought to produce pleasing ideas, and even if they are not bought, their ideas are thus used. Much rubbish has been written about the relationship between ideas and interests. Even Mannheim's *totaler Ideologieverdacht* (total suspicion of ideology) raises merely the question: so what? The fact that ideas can be looked at as interest-related does not tell us anything about their truth or falsehood, value or valuelessness (Merton: 'To consider how and how far social structures canalize the direction of scientific research is not to arraign the scientist for his motives');[1] and if there is a *total* suspicion of ideology, we may as well discount it. While it makes sense in moral terms to consider one's interest position if one produces ideas – and while we shall argue below that the producer of ideas has a degree of responsibility for abuses of his ideas – this kind of analysis is an open-ended game for those who enjoy it and yields little for social analysis.

The third starting point of the literature is the set of questions around the conditions under which ideas are generated. This is sometimes misleadingly called 'sociology of science', or 'sociology of art' (or even *Soziologie der Weltanschauungen*), for it is clearly of much more general interest. It is the lifelong subject of Robert K. Merton's imaginative and insightful scholarship.

All of these approaches are related to the question of the 'men of ideas' and their position to which we shall turn presently.

There is an important passage in *The Self and Its Brain* in which Karl Popper makes the point which we have in mind with characteristic fervour. I refer to it with almost total agreement. In a striking deduction (which he soaks in *Verfremdung* by using terms which are neither familiar nor likely to become familiar), Popper distinguishes the 'universe of physical entities' (World 1), the 'world of mental states' (World 2), and the 'world of the contents of thought and, indeed, of the products of the human mind' (World 3), and says about the latter (which alone is relevant for us at this point): 'By World 3 I mean the world of the products of the human mind, such as stories, explanatory myths, tools, scientific theories (whether true or false), scientific problems, social institutions, and works of art. World 3 objects are of our own making, although they are not always the result of planned production by individual men.' There are important relations between the Worlds: 'Many World 3 objects exist in the form of material bodies, and belong in a sense to both World 1 and World 3. Examples are sculptures, paintings, and books, whether devoted to a scientific subject or to literature. A book is a physical object, and it therefore belongs to World 1; but what makes it a significant production of the human mind is its *content*, that which remains invariant in various copies and editions. And this content belongs to World 3.' Nor is the inter-relationship of Worlds merely static; World 3 has reality: 'As World 3 objects, they may induce men to produce other World 3 objects and, thereby, act on World 1; and interaction with World 1 – even indirect interaction – I regard as a decisive argument for calling a thing real.' Or, even more powerfully put: '(1) World 3 objects are abstract . . . but nonetheless real, for they are powerful tools for changing World 1. . . . (2) World 3 objects have an effect on World 1 only through human inter-vention, the intervention of their makers; more especially, through being grasped, which is a World 2 process, a mental process, or more precisely, a process in which World 2 and World 3 interact. (3) We therefore have to admit that both World 3 objects and the processes of World 2 are real. . . .'[2]

Who, then, lives in World 3? Before we give a positive answer, the negative answer has to be considered: not everyone. We all do things, and thus live in World 1. We all feel things, and thus live in World 2. But we do not all create scientific theories, works of art, philosophical ideas. It may be that every man has an occasional and fleeting part in World 3: understanding God, re-thinking meaning, possibly producing a little poem for the beloved, a drawing, an explanation of something new. But even if this is so, it does not detract from the fact that the active and systematic life in World 3 is confined to a few. Not everyone creates new ideas.

I mention this as a fact, not as an objective. Many would share Popper's scorn about 'the morality of those who, being political or intellectual aristocrats, have a chance of getting into the textbooks of history'.[3] There is no reason to believe that producing ideas is a 'positional good' (in the sense of Fred Hirsch):[4] it is neither impossible to think of many, or even all people producing ideas, nor would it by itself detract from the value of ideas if everyone had them. Thus, why not fish in the morning, hunt in the afternoon (World 1), engage in critical criticism at night (World 3), and feel sick or happy about this life, as the case may be (World 2)?

There is a more difficult point here to which I can only allude; it has to do with quality. There is nothing wrong with encouraging creativity; the spark in every man and woman has to be kindled. But there is something wrong with a value system which no longer permits identifying quality. If the emphasis is on creativity rather than creation, on painting rather than the painting, writing rather than the book, then the emergence of ideas becomes that much more difficult, the genuinely new becomes the needle in the haystack, and fashion is likely to prevail over significance. Somehow the borderline has to be established between passive or reproductive World 3 activities, and active exploration of the open frontier of World 3. To quote Camus, 'the number of bad novels must not make us forget the value of the best.'[5] This requires ligatures, or linkages, that most precarious feature of modern societies which alone upholds standards. One of the strangest of all unfavourable conditions of creativity is thus the condition of universal claims to creativity. But we leave this paradox on one side here.

Even if we allow that the distinction between Popper's first two Worlds and World 3 is not in principle one between different people – that there is no intrinsic, or *a priori* 'class' structure corresponding to the Worlds – this much remains clear: that no one can live in World 3 all the time. Even the monk, let alone the university professor, will occasionally *do* and even *feel* things. More than that, most will spend the greater part of their lives in Worlds 1 and 2. There is something special about World 3, which is why it requires special attention.

World 3 activities are special in two senses: they provide a special opportunity (of exploration, innovation), and they require a special responsibility (of adding to the store of possible futures). There is something about these activities which gives them a status quite different from all others. They are carried out *on behalf* of people, in order to keep futures open *for* them. They are (as we shall say) representative activities.

The notion needs elaboration. I take it from the German philosopher Josef König.[6] The context is important. In a paper written in 1953, I had argued that freedom meant autonomous human activity, and that as such there was no difference between the dignity and significance of different activities, whether philosophical reflection, football playing, or stamp collecting. König did not like this much and replied (in a letter) with the following moving thought.

I would so much like to add a word about 'autonomy'. Of course I understand it with reference to Kant, and yet – in intention at least – not in a narrow Kantian sense. It somehow pretends something of a general validity. One may regard philosophizing or, e.g. being an artist as a hobby, like playing football or collecting stamps. And at heart I always feel embarrassed to get money for it. And yet I think at the same time that it is not a hobby – but in essence more than that. There is νόμος in it, and in νόμος there seems to lie something general. Thus I find that one would not express oneself correctly, if one were to say for example, 'I have made it "my law" to go for an hour's walk in the evening' (or for 'going for a walk', for example, 'playing football'). It also makes no sense, or so it seems to me, to say for example: he who plays football, or collects stamps, is doing this *representatively* for all others. But for philosophizing, or being an artist, this strange 'representative' quality might be valid on the understanding that only he does it in the right manner who does it 'representatively'. In this way, one might perhaps explicate the νόμος character in 'aut*onomy*'. In this way I might perhaps even understand being paid for it, although such understanding does not remove the embarrassment of being paid. This might perhaps become the beginning of another reflection. But if I veered towards it, my thoughts would become confused. One can feel in such moments like a sailing boat which anticipates the gales into which it is running, and which sees itself drifting keel-up before this has actually happened. I believe: one must never oneself want to be *certain* of doing something that one is doing, *representatively*.

The idea is not new, of course, and its history might well be written with profit. From Aristotle to Nietzsche and beyond it has appeared in many versions. The distinction between a βίος εωρήτικος, a life of theory and reflection, and a βίος πράκτικος, a life of practice and action, corresponds in important respects to that between representative, or World 3 activities, and all other human activities concerning Worlds 1 and 2. The point to be emphasized above all is the need for humility; it is here that the almost tortured, deeply serious conclusion of Josef König's argument seems to me a model. We must not even think the thought of representative activities unless we include in it the notion that doing things on behalf of others is a duty and responsibility, not a privilege and distinction. Moreover, no one can say of himself that he is engaged in representative activities; this is a judgment for others – and one supposes, not for contemporaries – to make.

This is not the place to begin to write the history to which I have alluded. But the point about humility is so important that there may be a case for quoting three representative authors (and thus incidentally adding to the understanding of representative activities).

Aristotle clearly saw a rank order between the theoretical and the practical life. His companion distinction between work and leisure is in fact an early expression of a persistent *topos* which regards work as inferior to non-work. There are places (in his *Politics*) where Aristotle seems to argue that the many have to work in order to give the few the chance of leisure. (This is, needless to say, what has happened in many periods of history.) In his *Nicomachean Ethics*, however, Aristotle is rather more subtle and differentiates. Happiness, he says, is activity which brings out man's capacities; greatest happiness is brought by the development of man's best capacities, those of insight, of εωρία. It is the only activity which is not sought for the sake of something else. 'We are assuming moreover that happiness must be mixed with pleasure; and the most pleasurable among the forms of activities of high value is admittedly the lively work of the philosophical mind. At any rate it holds for philosophy that it provides a pleasure which is magnificent by its purity and permanence. And it is for good reason that he who operates on the basis of his insights has a more pleasurable existence than he who is only seeking the ways that lead to them,' to say nothing of those who are 'incapable of happiness'. But Aristotle adds that no one can enjoy such happiness forever except the gods who have given man but a tiny share of their pleasures.[7]

An extreme expression of the arrogance of representative activities can be found in Nietzsche. 'A people,' he says, 'is the detour of nature in order to get to six, seven great men. – Yes: and in order then to get around them.' Another of his aphorisms is even more relevant in our context: 'Mankind does not constitute a development to the better or stronger or higher in the way in which this is believed today. "Progress" is merely a modern idea, that is to say, a false idea. . . . In another sense there is the persistent success of individual cases at the most varied places of the earth and within the most varied cultures, within which indeed a *higher type* presents itself: something which in relation to mankind as a whole is a superman (*Übermensch*).'[8]

Albert Camus likes to quote Nietzsche, but is in fact much closer to Josef König's (and our) view, and he puts it beautifully:

One of the temptations of the artist is to believe himself solitary, and in truth he hears this shouted at him with a certain base delight. But this is not true. He stands in the midst of all, in the same rank, neither higher nor lower, with all those who are working and struggling. His very vocation, in the face of oppression, is to open the prisons and to give a voice to the sorrows and joys of all. This is where art, against its enemies, justifies itself by proving precisely that it is no one's enemy. By itself art could probably not produce the renaissance which implies justice and liberty. But without it the renaissance would be without forms and, consequently, would be nothing. Without culture, and the relative freedom it implies, society, even when perfect, is but a jungle. This is why any authentic creation is a gift to the future.[9]

Representative activities then are about producing the content of new and different things – theories, works of art, kinds of life chances. They constitute the reservoir of possible futures. Without them, there can be no progress, though with them, progress is not guaranteed. Thus representative activities are both indispensable and wasteful. Whoever tries to curtail them will get stuck in the morass of existing insufficiencies, though whoever deliberately promotes them will be exposed to the discomforts of the not-yet (*das Noch-Nicht*, a term of Ernst Bloch's that seems preferable to the spirit of Utopia).[10] Relevant or not, there is a sense in which the creative potential of representative activities shows man at his best.

Inevitably, discussion of representative activities is reflection, consideration of the position and work of the scientist or the artist. What am I doing in writing a piece of philosophical analysis? The same is true, of course, for Aristotle's justification of the theoretical life, and it is hard not to suppose that Nietzsche regarded himself as one of those fortunate incidents which make whole peoples worth while. Other theories require other, often more elaborate constructions. If there is assumed to be an inevitable Path of History, it becomes more difficult to explain the communion of its discoverer with the World Spirit: 'At times at which the class struggle approaches a decision, the process of dissolution within the ruling class, within the entire old society, takes on such an intense, glaring character, that a part of the ruling class abandons it and joins the revolutionary class . . . and especially a part of the bourgeois ideologists who have worked their way up to an understanding of the entire historical process'.[11] Even Karl Mannheim has to use much skill to find a place for himself in a world of 'total ideological suspicion', and invent a 'free-floating intelligentsia' whose members have experienced so many breaks with their primary groups that their thinking is no longer unambiguously determined by class allegiances.[12]

Those who are professionally engaged in representative activities (who get paid for them) are evidently of special interest.
They include several different types even apart from consisting,
by definition, of many different individuals. Some pursue *l'art
pour l'art*, following an inner drive, attempting *rerum cognoscere
causas*, seeking truth; there are many ways in which this has been
put. Then there are the legitimizers, those who provide the
material for those in power, help them do their job, explain
what they are doing to others; advisers, planners, public relations people, and the like. Further, there are the rebels, the
sociologists who seek what is not – not yet – institution. And of
course there are the jesters, hard to pin down, hard to live with,
the journalists perhaps, the critics from the sidelines. The
distinctions are theoretical. People's motives do not necessarily
coincide with their actions, let alone their effects. But the distinctions are useful as a warning against simple generalization.

There is one conspicuous omission in the catalogue of representative activities which we have incidentally given so far, that
is, the politician or statesman. (*Mutatis mutandis*, what we shall
say applies to other leaders as well, whether in business, or
organizations of any kind; but for reasons of brevity we shall
concentrate on responsibility for the political community.) The
omission is all the more striking since politicians – at least,
though by no means only under conditions of 'representative
government' – are the one group which explicitly describes its
activity as one on behalf of others. Nevertheless, the omission is
no accident. Whatever its distinction and significance, political
activity is not representative in the strict sense of World 3
activities. Politics is not undertaken on behalf of others who
could and would not do it, but with respect to others who have
certain more or less articulate demands; it is not representative,
but (as we shall call it) legitimative.

These are subtle distinctions, and not value judgments. No
implicit or explicit criterion for regarding politics or arts and
sciences as more valuable is suggested here. But we may wish to
distinguish between Worlds 3a and 3b, or even introduce a
World 3/2, considering Max Weber's understandable demand

F

for 'passion' as well as a 'sense of proportion and responsibility' in the politician.[13] Sometimes, triteness helps: politics is the art of the possible; representative activities are the grasp for the stars. Political representatives, if they are not of the irrelevant kind that aims for nothing but high support figures in opinion polls, try to drag the indolent mass of status quo views as far ahead of itself as possible; but both moral and practical legitimacy remain crucial. They have to give reasons for what they are doing, and they have to carry the people. The good politician always has one eye on objectives and the other on support. He may strain the latter a bit if the objective is particularly important; he may also forget about the former for a while if his support is flagging. In that sense politics is impure, a balancing act which at best moves the centre of the equilibrium a little forward, and at worst leaves everything as it is. There is no doubt about the creativity of politics; but it is different in quality from that of the poet and the philosopher. In Josef König's terms, one might say that there is every reason why the politician should be paid, however much one may doubt the salary of the professor. (That modern societies tend to take the opposite view is worth another reflection, taking into account how recent the phenomenon is: Bismarck still got large sums of money for his victories whereas Marx was not the only intellectual who would have been starving without a Maecenas.) Insofar as politics is representative, this describes a straightforward relationship to a constituency which demands legitimation. Legitimation on the other hand is a term which does not arise for representative activities in our sense; they involve something that is totally removed from most people, and even of doubtful relevance, but nevertheless an expression of human possibilities which must be more than a source of personal pleasure to those engaged in it.

Much could be added to these elliptic remarks. For instance, there may be great statesmen – visionary politicians – who straddle the boundary between representative and legitimative activities. The place of political theorists has to be considered also. We shall return to the 'straddlers' a little later. Again, the subject has a long history. Aristotle was sufficiently ambiguous on the role of the politician to allow Hannah Arendt to ascribe to him many of the qualities which we have confined to representative activities here.[14] In fact, Aristotle invented a kind of World 3/2: while politics is clearly not a form of theoretical life, it is not the practical life in the sense of the toil of the slave either; it is a distinguished mixture. On what happens, if the two vocations of science and of politics become professions as well (*Beruf*, in the double meaning of the German word), Max Weber had some important things to say in the two Munich lectures of 1920.[15] He was clearly right to single out these two human activities, whose explosive relationship accounts for so much in human history.

Representative and legitimative activities are unlike all other activities of men in that their combination accounts for what may be called progress in human affairs. Representative activities create the horizon of possibilities which accompanies social life, whether as the not-yet or the never. Legitimative activities shape reality by borrowing from the horizon of possibilities those items which are both desirable and capable of being implemented, given the circumstances of action. In reality, of course, this sweet division of labour is much less simple. When the great Austrian actor and theatre director Max Reinhardt died in exile in 1943, in the middle of the war, one of his eulogists said: 'At a time at which political struggles demand a clear position from the theatre, one has taken offence at the fact that the great actor had no sense for the so-called political theatre.' At that time at least, this may well have been the only defensible form of representative activities, because legitimative activities, at least in the country from which Reinhardt was exiled, aimed entirely at maintaining morally reprehensible power. Thus it would have been difficult to invent for the cynical and brutal politics of absolute power such justifications as Max Reinhardt's eulogist could plausibly offer: 'But his theatre was political in a higher sense, by being able to gather and unite what could no longer find itself on any other plane in its space of common contemplation.'[16]

We are concerned here with representative activities. Legitimative activities figure merely as a mirror in which they are reflected, or perhaps the non-identical twin who brings out the differences more clearly than any abstract description. For the relationship between the two activities is a privileged one. It will therefore accompany us as we look at what may be called the social structure of representative activities: the norms and sanctions that govern them; the relationship of these norms to those of society at large; and the institutions which accommodate the doll within the doll, that is, the norms of representative activities within those of the larger society.

The fact is puzzling and notable that those engaged in representative activities find themselves subject to a morality all of their own. If it is said that 'this hypothesis is not testable', or 'that conjecture fails to take account of Virgil's use of the word', or 'he has broken the style of the introductory chapters and become unsure of his manner of expression', such judgments may have devastating effects. To be sure, the same is true if a Rotarian fails to attend sixty per cent of the meetings of his club, or if a Social Democrat does not pay his party dues for a year. But there is a difference. The private rules of clubs and organizations emulate the social contract for limited ranges of social positions; they are in an important sense like social laws or norms. As a result, transgressions are explicitly sanctioned; the Rotarian is expelled, membership of the Social-Democratic Party lapses. In the case of representative activities, on the other hand, norms are self-sanctioning in the sense that the desired result cannot be achieved unless they are complied with. This is what Josef König may have meant when he spoke of doing representative activities 'in the right manner'. In principle, the rules of the Rotary Club or the Social Democratic Party are arbitrary; they could be different, although in the given form they serve to constitute the organizations as they are. The same cannot be said for the rules of the game of scientific discovery or artistic invention. Scientists and artists may form clubs with Rotarian or Social Democratic rules – one cannot be a professor without having a Ph.D.; one cannot be a member of PEN without having published at least one book; etc. – but this concerns them as scientific and artistic citizens. The process of discovery and invention itself is subject to rules which are not arbitrary, even though they themselves may develop as discovery progresses. They are, in other words, an independent, separate morality.

The puzzling aspect of this morality is that it is not general. Whereas moral values, like laws, in principle apply to everybody, the morality of representative activities does not. If, say, a politician develops what to all intents and purposes is an untestable hypothesis in conversation with his colleagues, it does not make the slightest difference to him or anybody else whether it is testable or not. If a civil servant writes a paper incorporating contributions from several others, it is entirely irrelevant that the style is syncretistic, or even abominable. People are subject to the morality of representative activities only if and insofar as they engage in them; even then, they can opt out without telling anybody, or being told by anybody about it. The ethics of discovery and invention is in one sense the most voluntary of all; though for those who have chosen to submit to it, it becomes more compelling than any set of Rotarian or Social-Democratic rules, or even public laws.

The phenomenon of the ethics of scientific discovery (as *pars pro toto*) requires explanation, say, in terms of the uncertainty of the human condition; we shall not pursue this line of analysis here. Given the human condition, and notably the social contract, it is not surprising that people have tried throughout history to crystallize the morality of discovery and invention and create institutions around it, academies; we shall look at an aspect of this phenomenon presently. But first it is necessary to consider briefly the relationship between the ethics of representative activities (the logic of scientific discovery, the rules of artistic invention), and the morality of social life. The issue has been given many names. Recently, 'theory and practice' or, more esoterically, 'praxis', has become fashionable again. Between the present and the last fashion of this terminology, 'social science and value judgments' was an emotional version of the same issue. With respect to the arts, the question often arose more dramatically still, if less theoretically: what if the artist says or represents things which are shocking, objectionable, unacceptable to the moral community around him? He is censored, arrested, exiled, of course; but the underlying issue is the same conflict between the morality of representative activities and the morality of the social and political community.

Again there is, of course, a vast literature on the subject. Perhaps, a methodological remark is in place at this point. One may dispute the value of eighteenth-century style think pieces like this at a time at which most things have been said somehow, and concern with highly technical issues is the order of the day. I respect this view, though I disagree. One of the characteristics of the present state of knowledge is an abundance of information which makes it virtually impossible to see the wood for the trees. This information is valuable, indeed indispensable; it is the task of scholars and others engaged in representative activities to recognize and channel the existing stream of information. But it is an equally important and indispensable task to try and cut through the tangle (as we have put it earlier) and make sense of issues by returning to the sources. There are certain simple problems which remain such even if they are covered by seemingly endless layers of books and articles of reflection and re-reflection. The problem of theory and practice is one of them, and we shall try to state its simple structure without reference to the literature (except for one quotation).

Marx's Eleventh thesis on Feuerbach is substantially silly, politically dangerous, yet a useful starting point for the analysis of the relationship between philosophy and politics: 'Philosophers have merely interpreted the world differently; what matters is to change it.'[17] The thesis is false in at least three major respects; and these define the three principles which govern the relationship between representative and legitimative activities, theory and praxis.

'Philosophers have merely interpreted the world differently.' There is no philosopher, however conventional, limited, or second-rate, who had set out to interpret the world 'differently'. Incidents of forced originality or the attempt to be different (as one suspects them in modern art sometimes) apart, philosophy, science and art are after truth. They cannot achieve it; whatever we do by way of representing the world is but an approximation, and often of melancholy imperfection; but about the attempt and its motive there can be no doubt. Far from being a cause for scorn, the differences in interpretation of the world are a testimony to the honest search for progress. Given uncertainty, that is, the constitutional inability of men to find the grail of truth, or at any rate to know that they have found it, difference and plurality are part and parcel of the moral world of discovery and invention. Where there is no difference, the values of representative activities have been violated. Marx may have dreamt of a society which is so perfect that it provides the real basis for a perfect superstructure of philosophy; but in the real world claims of perfection can be maintained only at the cost of suppression.

'What matters is to change it.' It is of course misleading to discuss one Marxian statement out of context. Marx was too much of a philosopher himself to wish to disparage philosophy as such; and when he talks of change almost as a purpose in itself, in the cynical libertarian manner of Hayek's 'movement for movement's sake',[18] we must not forget that he had a notion of its direction and underlying laws of development. Nevertheless, the disjunction of philosophy and politics has to be rejected. The esoteric morality of representative activities means among other things that there is no telling what the practical effect will be if an artist, scientist, philosopher sets out on his course. There may be no effect at all; there may be a fundamental, for instance, a 'Copernican' change in perspective; there may be a delayed and distorted effect like the application of Montesquieu's *Esprit de Lois* to the American constitution; there may be the kind of almost direct translation characteristic of certain areas of scientific research today. In any case, those involved in legitimative activities, in shaping reality, not only need 'philosophy' in order to adumbrate their actions, but also in order to give them a sense of direction. Changing the world without an idea of direction, that is, without applying discoveries, is at best a benevolent *acte gratuite*; in fact it sounds more like the anti-philosophy of fascism, of stalinism, and of terrorism.

The two moralities then stand in a significantly oblique relationship to each other. The values of reasonable politics require the attempt to find out what can be found out about future direction. It was unreasonable, after Keynes, to ignore the possibilities of demand management in economic policy. The values of reasonable science, on the other hand, require the attempt to disparage and supersede whatever is the established doctrine. It would have been unreasonable for economists after Keynes to breathe a sigh of relief and turn to other things; they had to wonder when and why demand management does not work. For the politician, this is confusing. He may well be tempted to turn to Marx's thesis and discount those 'philosophers' who come up with new solutions all the time. Only the most sophisticated societies understand that imposing the values of the moral community on representative activities inevitably destroys their opportunities. This is the case for the proverbial long leash on which theory must be held by practitioners, the need for patience among those who want to apply knowledge.

For those engaged in representative activities, the oblique relationship between their values and those of the moral community to which they also belong is even more painful. When Karl Popper received equally enthusiastic congratulatory addresses from conservative and socialist politicians on the occasion of his seventy-fifth birthday, he remained unworried; everybody knew his views anyway, he argued.[19] He may be right; but the problem is more difficult. The Oppenheimer dilemma is a dramatic case in point. All modern scientists have experienced the possibility that by following their values they increase the potential of evil in the real world. Social scientists on the other hand, in their eagerness to do good, have looked more at relevance in terms of the general moral values of their societies than at compliance with the ethics of scientific discovery; as a result, they have produced endless rubbish. Put in this way, the dilemma is almost incapable of solution: Ignore society, and your value-free science may lend itself to terrible abuse; embrace society, and your value-laden science will become plainly bad.

Is there an answer to the dilemma? Perhaps not, or only in an ideal world. The theoretical answer is that being engaged in representative activities involves a special responsibility, an awareness of implications. Systems of self-control with respect to biological research that may lead to genetic manipulation; or insistence by nuclear scientists that as much money must be spent on nuclear safety as on reactor construction, are practical examples of this responsibility.[20] But there is no instance or agency which can enforce such responsibility. Scientists will do research which can be abused, and philosophers will advance ideas which can be used to legitimize evil. Politicians and other practitioners, on the other hand, will take whatever they can find to advance their objectives; these may be honest and good, or they may be dishonest and evil. In the process, and to make matters worse, some politicians will pretend that their policies are scientific, and some scientists will fancy themselves as having dialectically reconciled theory and practice. It is a confused world, and those in representative activities may enlighten it, but will not save it.

We have distinguished representative and legitimative activities, and discussed some of the confusions arising from the oblique relationship of their values; but increasingly there is a group of people who *straddle* the two worlds. 'Philosophy' stretches out its hand in the form of 'policy studies', that is research which accepts the subject preferences and time scales of the practitioner. 'Change' on the other hand stretches out its hand by adding planning sections and think tanks to government departments. (*Mutatis mutandis* the same happens in business and wherever decisions are taken.) It is doubtful whether the two hands actually meet – inquiry and action will forever follow different norms – but in the process a group emerges which feels equally at home in both worlds, scientific politicians, political scientists, advisers, planners. In most countries this is still an uneasy group which feels (rightly to some extent) that it is not recognized by either side, and whose members therefore develop ambitions either to get a university chair or a parliamentary seat. In some countries, the group of straddlers is beginning to be large enough to develop its own consciousness. This is not an easy process, even in theory, as we have seen; and it may never succeed. It is therefore not meant to be Platonic if we suggest that the kind of responsibility to which we have alluded might well be the predominant value of the straddler group: since they understand (presumably) both the requirements of scientific discovery and those of legitimate action, they can see the pitfalls in the relation of the two more clearly than others. A code of conduct for the straddlers themselves would almost by definition be an explication of the principles of responsibility with respect to the uneasy relationship of science and politics, representative and legitimative activities. There is a programme here for the representatives of the Brookings Institution and the American Enterprise Institute and other institutions of this kind.

All institutions perish by their victories (to follow Renan), but none more rapidly and thoroughly than those designed to gather representative activities. Yet at least some and perhaps all representative activities need institutions almost as much as we all need society. 'Big science' may be straddling as often as it is creative; but it needs institutes and expensive equipment in any case. Philosophers (in the widest pre-nineteenth century sense) at the very least need someone to talk to, and probably some kind of master-disciple relationship, even if the modern ideology demands calling it by other names (colleagues, *Mitarbeiter*). The 'scientific community' *à la* Kuhn is both a useful fiction and an organizational reality, albeit one that rarely lives up to its moral function. The social history of art is full of instances of institutionalization, from Maecenas to the Ford Foundation, and of course of actual institutions, Bloomsbury, the *Bauhaus*. These institutions (I said) are *almost* as necessary as society. Men cannot survive without society; but representative activities ultimately transcend all boundaries of organization and institution. They are by their very nature unbounded. Whatever their institutional eggshells may be, they struggle and then fly away from them to endless horizons of truth and of beauty.

The ideal-typical institution of and for representative activities is the academy, Ἀκαδεμία. This must not be confused with 'academic' institutions in the modern sense, universities. It is true that in the nineteenth century a notion of the 'idea of the university' had become fashionable which lingers on among the more abstrusely idealistic scholars of the present (or perhaps those defending an interest in remoteness?), and which claims for universities the exclusive right to house those engaged in representative activities. It is also true that universities, through the ages, have given asylum to some of them, notably in the *artium facultates* of the Middle Ages, more generally in the new nineteenth-century university of Europe and, later, its Anglo-American version, the Graduate School. But in all essential respects universities have always been training institutions; a place for straddlers at best, for craftsmen as often. This is clearly true for the old faculties of theology, medicine and law; it is equally clearly true for the mass education institutions of the late twentieth century. Josef König was paid for this function of his work, not for the enjoyment of representative activity. The university is in some respects the modern, democratic version of the old aristocratic family which kept a distinguished, sometimes brilliant *Hauslehrer* to take the young brats to Italy and to the delights of Cicero and Euclid. He was bored, of course, but at least he earned a living, and even met some interesting people in the process, so that he could write his *Leviathan* or *Monadenlehre* all the more effectively.

Representative activities can be threatened by bans as well as by institutionalization. Indeed, in the modern world the choice is often between the Lubjanka and the iron cage of bondage of a bureaucratized university institute. The academy lives, under such conditions, in the interstices, in *samizdat* circles, in structureless groups like the *Gruppe 47* of German writers, or the *Bourbaki* group of French mathematicians, and in meeting places like the Center for Advanced Study in Palo Alto. Never has as much money been spent on the arts and sciences as in the second half of the twentieth century; and yet one wonders whether there is any increase at all in the creative discoveries and inventions by representative activity. The academy is a fleeting institution with a limited lifespan; a bureaucratized world favours permanent prisons of ideas. The academy is an institution in which only ideas count, and some are clearly better than others; a democratized world favours the equality of all professors. The academy is bound to be outrageous at times and critical of established doctrine at all times; modern societies do not like the discomforts of doubt any more than their predecessors, even if they have found more subtle means of protecting themselves.

The figure of analysis with which we began this reflective chapter is in one respect incomplete. Man is imperfect and his condition wrought with uncertainty. We are therefore seeking ourselves, or perhaps seeking ways of improving human nature through the social conditions of life. The means by which this is done is conflict. There appears to be an eternal antagonism between what is, and what could be, social institutions and social forces. Class conflicts and political struggles express this antagonism. Such conflicts are not empty battles, senseless heroism like the First World War of 1914; they are about human life chances. New life chances can be discovered. Their emergence is in the first instance a matter of ideas, of discoveries and inventions. Legitimative activities need the results of representative activities to define the direction of change. Representative activities provide meaning and goals. But they provide something else as well, hope; and without hope there is no progress.

In the analysis of revolution, it has often been pointed out that a revolutionary situation is not enough. However defined, revolutionary situations are more frequent than revolutions. Nor does it make sense to assume (with Marx) that the probability, even necessity of revolution increases as the revolutionary situation becomes more extreme. On the contrary, extreme deprivation produces lethargy. What is needed to turn a revolutionary situation into revolution is the spark that sets fire to an explosive mixture of socio-chemicals. This spark is hope. It consists in part in the apparent weakness of those in power; most revolutions are preceded by the rulers of the day beginning to give way. But this is merely the negative side. The positive side is some idea of what may be after the revolution, hope, in the form of an image of the future.

Revolutionary hopes are invariably disappointed. The moment of extreme freedom is soon followed by a new tyranny. Revolutionary hope is generally utopian and thus the stuff from which inhuman and unchecked power is made. Yet the figure of analysis has (as we have argued before) general application. Change requires flexible institutions, capable of adjustment without disruption. But change also requires a prospect, a design into the future, an idea of where one might go. Such ideas are provided by those engaged in representative activities. 'Any authentic creation is a gift to the future.' Without the emergence of new ideas by representative activities, societies become truly hope-less, drab, grey and profoundly miserable. It is useful to remember this at a time at which progress only too often seems to favour such drabness and destroy the opportunities of hope.

Notes

While the chapters of this volume were not all conceived for the purpose, their subject is the same and they were all written after my Reith Lectures (*The New Liberty*) in 1975. The central parts of the volume were in fact written between the Christian Gauss Lectures which I gave at Princeton University in March 1977 and the Lionel Trilling Seminar at Columbia University in December 1978. (The title of both was *Life Chances*.) About half the present text has not been published anywhere before. Notes on particular chapters contain the relevant information about their history. Here, the general point is worth mentioning that even published texts have been reconsidered for the present volume, and some have been changed considerably before inclusion.

I have indicated the intellectual context of the pieces in this volume in the Preface. One further remark of textual biography, however, may be in place. Chapters 1 and 3, that is almost half the volume, consist largely of texts which I have set aside in another context. In preparing a larger work on the twilight of the modern world ('Modernity in Eclipse', perhaps), I have made half a dozen theoretical approaches and written some two hundred pages before there emerged a fifty-page chapter which will be found, I hope, in my book in the near future. The reason for such self-control, not to say self-criticism, was partly the insufficiency of early drafts, but partly also the fact that the book on modernity is one of analysis rather than theory. The opposite is true for the present volume.

In the more distant future I am planning to publish a series of working papers on theoretical matters. In a sense, this is one of these working papers, although it has become a little too long for my liking: Paul Maas's little volume on textual criticism has remained a model for me of how theory should be presented. However, the author at least is pleased about the unsystematic character of this volume, because this makes it possible to fill the arid emptiness of conceptual discussion in a colourful way with apparently irrelevant material and thus make it palatable.

The various pieces are full of allusions. References are included in these notes only where such allusions are explicit.

Chapter One
Anything New Under the Sun? On the Meaning of History and the Possibility of Progress

This is for the most part one of the texts which I have dismissed in the context of the book on modernity; it has been supplemented and re-worked for this volume.

[1] Homer, *Iliad*, I, 69.

[2] Concepts of F. Hirsch, *Social Limits to Growth* (London 1977).

[3] K. Marx, *Theses on Feuerbach*, p. 11. Thesis.

[4] I take this distinction from my teacher, the philosopher Josef König, who has used it in lectures and seminars. In the Reith Lectures (*The New Liberty*, London 1975), I used the words *problem* and *question* the other way round (following advice by my BBC producer). I now regret this, for 'problem' is naturally further from common usage than 'question'. It may be useful to mention, however, that the use of the words is not likely to be consistent in this volume; consistency would be unnecessarily artificial.

[5] H. Giersch, *Allgemeine Wirtschaftspolitik* (Wiesbaden 1960), p. 97. My translation.

[6] Cf. K. Jaspers, *Die grossen Philosophen* (München 1957).

[7] *Ecclesiastes, or The Preacher*, I, 1, 10.

[8] Personal communication from Sir Karl Popper, 13 November 1977.

[9] K. R. Popper and J. C. Eccles, *The Self and Its Brain* (New York-London–Berlin 1977), p. 22. For a more elaborate discussion of World 3, see also below, p. 144.

[10] There are many versions of this distinction in modal logics, such as (with Aristotle) 'unilateral' and 'bilateral possibility', or 'indeterminate' and 'natural possibility' (cf., e.g. I. M. Bochenski, *Formale Logik*, Freiburg-München 1956, p. 94 *et seq.*).

[11] Popper and Eccles, *The Self and Its Brain*, p. 25.

[12] K. R. Popper, *The Open Society and Its Enemies* (London 1952), p. 269 *et seq.*

[13] G. W. F. Hegel, *Grundlinien der Philosophie des Rechts*, § 358. My translation.

[14] W. Schulz, *Philosophie in der veränderten Welt* (Pfullingen 1972), p. 612. My translation.

[15] I. Kant, *Idee zu einer allgemeinen Geschichte in weltbürgerlicher Absicht*, Eighth Proposition. My translation.

[16] Hegel, *Grundlinien* . . . , Preface. My translation.

[17] Kant, *Idee* . . . , Fourth Proposition. The preceding remarks are a nuanced paraphrase of Kant's argument.

[18] Ibid.

[19] R. Koselleck, 'Fortschritt', in *Geschichtliche Grundbegriffe – Historisches Lexikon zur politisch-sozialen Sprache in Deutschland* (Stuttgart 1976), p. 375. My translation.

[20] F. Engels, 'Die Lage Englands. Die englische Konstitution', in *Marx-Engels-Werke*, I, p. 578. My translation.

[21] Letter to Danielson in *Marx-Engels-Werke*, XXXVIII, p. 363. My translation.

[22] D. Bell, *The Cultural Contradictions of Capitalism* (New York 1976), p. 165 *et seq.*

[23] This is an allusion to B. Snell, *Die Entdeckung des Geistes* (Hamburg 1948).

[24] Cf. above, n. 9.

[25] Kant, *Idee* . . . , Third Proposition.

Chapter Two
Life Chances. Dimensions of Liberty in Society

For the most part, this is the text of the lecture which I gave on the occasion of the Lionel Trilling Seminar at Columbia University, New York, on 7 December 1978. The lecture was drafted with a view to this volume. At one important point, I have extended and changed the text of the lecture; this includes the substitution of 'ligatures' for 'connexions'.

[1] B. Brecht, *Dreigroschenoper*, III, 7. My translation.

[2] J. S. Mill, 'Utilitarianism', in *Utilitarianism, Liberty and Representative Government* (London 1910), p. 6.

[3] Aristotle, *Nicomachean Ethics*, quotations from I, 2–10.

⁴ Cf. Government of Czechoslovak Soviet Socialist Republic (ORBIS): *The Right to Happiness* (Prague 1965), p. 2.

⁵ R. A. Easterlin, 'Does Economic Growth Improve the Human Lot?', in P. A. David and M. Reder (eds.), *Nations and Households in Economic Growth* (Stanford 1972).

⁶ Cf. G. Gallup, 'What Mankind Thinks About Itself', in *Readers Digest*, CIX (October 1976).

⁷ Cf. F. A. von Hayek, *The Constitution of Liberty* (London 1960), p. 41; and Popper, *The Open Society and Its Enemies*, Chapter 25.

⁸ L. Trilling, *The Liberal Imagination* (New York 1957), p. x.

⁹ W. L. Davidson, *Political Thought in England* (London 1915), p. 15.

¹⁰ V. Pareto, *Traité de Sociologie Générale* (Lausanne–Paris 1917), § 2111.

¹¹ J. Bentham, *The Principles of Morals and Legislation*, Chapter I, III.

¹² Bentham, *op cit*, Chapter IV with the famous memoriter verses ('intense, long, certain . . . ').

¹³ Mill, 'Utilitarianism', p. 11.

¹⁴ Giersch, *Allgemeine Wirtschaftspolitik*, p. 97. My translation.

¹⁵ R. A. Dahl and C. E. Lindblom, *Politics, Economics and Welfare* (New York 1953), p. 28 *et seq.*

¹⁶ L. Robbins, *Political Economy–Past and Present* (London 1976), p. 3 n.

¹⁷ T. B. Bottomore, *Elites and Society* (London 1964), p. 142.

¹⁸ Hirsch, *Social Limits to Growth*, p. 5.

¹⁹ M. Weber, *Wirtschaft und Gesellschaft* (Tübingen 1956), p. 20. All translations of quotes from Weber are mine.

²⁰ Cf. for these quotations from Weber, Chapter Three, IV, below.

²¹ See for further 'games' of this kind, Chapter Three, V, below.

²² R. K. Merton, 'Social Structure and Anomie', in *Social Theory and Social Structure* (rev. ed., Glencoe 1957), particularly p. 157 *et seq.*

²³ Trilling, *The Liberal Imagination*, p. x *et seq.*

²⁴ Popper, *The Open Society and Its Enemies*.

²⁵ References to R. Nozick, *Anarchy, State and Utopia* (Oxford 1974); several publications by J. Habermas, including *Rekonstruktion des historischen Materialismus* (Frankfurt 1976); J. Rawls; *A Theory of Justice* (Oxford 1972).

Chapter Three
Seven Notes on the Concept of Life Chances

The notes assembled in this chapter are all unpublished. They are taken from different contexts. Note IV (on Max Weber) was the starting point of my reflections on the subject of this volume; the present text has several layers, some of which reach back more than ten years. Notes II, III and to some extent VII are based on drafts for the Christian Gauss Lectures in Princeton 1977. The other notes have been written for this volume.

1 K. R. Popper, *The Logic of Scientific Discovery* (New York 1959), pp. 64 *et seq.*

2 This remark should be taken with a grain of salt in view of the fact that there is something slightly artificial about the chapter on 'Basic Concepts of Sociology' at the head of all editions of *Economy and Society*.

3 Cf. the quotation from Kant above, p. 20.

4 Nozick, *Anarchy, State and Utopia.*

5 A point made above all in conversations. Cf., however, the chapter on 'Social Welfare Measures', in *Capitalism and Freedom* (Chicago 1962).

6 In a discussion on French television with the president of the French Employers' Federation in the spring of 1974.

7 Cf. my paper on 'Sociology and the Sociologist', in *Essays in the Theory of Society* (London 1968).

8 G. Rudé, *The Crowd in the French Revolution* (Oxford 1959), p. 4.

9 R. Dahrendorf, *Class and Class Conflict in Industrial Society* (Stanford 1959).

10 Idem, p. 176.

11 Idem, ch. IV, as well as R. Dahrendorf, 'Karl Marx und die Theorie des sozialen Wandels', in *Pfade aus Utopia* (München 1967).

12 A. Toynbee, *Civilization on Trial* (London 1948).

13 All quotations in this paragraph from K. Marx, *Grundrisse der Kritik der politischen Ökonomie* (Moscow 1939/1941), p. 438 *et seq.* My translation.

14 Popper, *Open Society and Its Enemies.*

15 Kant, *Idee zu einer allgemeinen Geschichte in weltbürgerlicher Absicht*, Preface.

16 H. Schellhoss, 'Der Begriff der Chance bei Max Weber', in *Studien und Berichte aus dem Soziologischen Seminar der Universität Tübingen*, no. 1 (1963). K. F. Schumann, *Zeichen der Unfreiheit* (Freiburg 1968), especially p. 85 *et seq.* E. Siberski, *Untergrund*

und offene Gesellschaft (Stuttgart 1967), pp. 113–78. G. Hufnagel, *Kritik als Beruf* (Frankfurt-Berlin-Wien 1971), passim, cf. index.

[17] G. Hufnagel, *Kritik als Beruf*, p. 179.

[18] All quotations in the following section from the edition of Max Weber, *Wirtschaft und Gesellschaft* (Tübingen 1956); here p. 9.

[19] Idem., p. 29.

[20] Idem., p. 182.

[21] J. S. Mill, 'Utilitarianism', op. cit., p. 15.

[22] Weber, *Wirtschaft und Gesellschaft*, p. 181.

[23] Idem, p. 17.

[24] Idem, p. 184.

[25] Idem, p. 13.

[26] Idem, p. 23.

[27] Idem, p. 201.

[28] Idem, p. 34.

[29] Idem, p. 255.

[30] Idem, p. 266.

[31] Idem, p. 377.

[32] Idem, p. 47.

[33] Idem, p. 180.

[34] Idem, p. 167.

[35] Idem, p. 193.

[36] Idem, p. 28.

[37] Idem, p. 122.

[38] Idem, p. 123.

[39] Idem, p. 177.

[40] Idem, p. 20.

[41] Idem, p. 20.

[42] Idem, p. 21.

[43] Idem, p. 22.

[44] Idem, p. 22.

[45] Idem, p. 60.

[46] Professor William Barrett has justly emphasized this aspectin his comment on the Lionel Trilling Lecture (cf. Chapter 2 above).

[47] A. Smith, *Wealth of Nations*, Book III, Chapter I.

[48] Cf. H. H. Gerth and C. W. Mills, *Character and Social Structure* (New York 1953), especially Chapter II, 2.

[49] Merton, *Social Theory and Social Structure*, p. 147.

[50] Cf. E. Allardt, *About Dimensions of Welfare* (Helsinki 1973).

[51] Cf. in this connection D. E. Christian, 'International Social

Indicators: The OECD Experience', in *Social Indicators Research*, vol. 1 (1974).

52 Cf. W. Zapf and H. J. Krupp, *Sozialpolitik und Sozialberichterstattung* (Frankfurt 1977).

53 'Social Structure and Anomie', 'Continuities in the Theory of Social Structure and Anomie', both in Merton, *Social Theory and Social Structure*.

54 Idem, p. 162.

55 Idem, p. 134.

56 Idem, p. 135.

57 Idem, p. 162.

58 Idem, p. 161 *et seq.* Quotations from R. M. MacIver, *The Ramparts We Guard* (New York 1950), p. 84 *et seq.*

59 Idem, p. 176.

60 Idem, p. 177.

61 Idem, p. 162 *et seq.*

62 von Hayek, *The Constitution of Liberty*, p. 77.

63 K. Marx, *Das Kapital* (Berlin 1953), p. 8 3 *et seq.* My translation.

64 von Hayek, *The Constitution of Liberty*, p. 19.

Chapter Four
Liberalism

This was originally a dictionary article, which may still be noticeable. It was published in *Meyers Enzyklopädisches Lexikon*, vol. 15 (Mannheim 1974). I have included it here because it presents the elements of liberal political theories concisely and in the categories of this volume.

1 J. Locke, *The Second Treatise of Government*, II, 13.

2 von Hayek, *The Constitution of Liberty*, p. 34.

3 Cf. J. Habermas, *Strukturwandel der Öffentlichkeit* (Neuwied 1962).

4 Cf. Nozick, *Anarchy, State and Utopia*.

Chapter Five
The End of the Social-Democratic Consensus? The Legitimacy of Political Power in Contemporary Societies

This revised text of a lecture given at the European Forum in

Alpbach in 1978 is included here because it provides a link between theoretical considerations and empirical analysis. A shortened version will appear (in German) in the Proceedings of the Forum.

[1] J. Habermas, *Zur Rekonstruktion des historischen Materialismus* (Frankfurt 1976), p. 298.

[2] Idem, p. 298.

[3] Idem, p. 299.

[4] In her address to the party conference of the German Christian Democratic Union (CDU) in 1978.

[5] Cf. his contributions to M. Crozier, S. Huntington, J. Watanuki, *The Crisis of Democracy* (New York 1975).

[6] H. Arendt, *Vita Activa oder vom tätigen Leben* (Munich 1960).

[7] Hirsch, *Social Limits to Growth*.

Chapter Six
Inequality, Hope and rogress

This is the text of a lecture given originally on 24 February 1976 at the University of Manchester and published under this title (Liverpool 1976). For inclusion in this volume I have changed the text at several critical points.

[1] Cf. C. Jencks, *Inequality* (New York 1972); and Rawls, *A Theory of Justice*.

[2] E. Bloch, *Zur Ontologie des Noch-Nicht-Seins* (Frankfurt 1961).

[3] M. Ginsberg, *Reason and Unreason in Society* (London 1956); p. 298.

[4] Cf. T. H. Marshall, *Citizenship and Social Class* (Cambridge 1950).

[5] A more elaborate argument on the thesis developed up to this point can be found in my 'Liberty and Equality', in the *Essays in the Theory of Society* (London 1968).

[6] R. Dahrendorf, *Bildung ist Bürgerrecht* (Hamburg 1965).

[7] Jencks, *Inequality*, p. 8 *et seq.*

[8] Cf. D. Bell, *The Coming of Post-Industrial Society* (New York 1973), p. 408 *et seq.*, and espec ally the discussion of Rawls, p. 440 *et seq.*

[9] Cf. S. Huntington, in M. Crozier and others, *The Crisis of Democracy*; and R. Heilbroner, *An Inquiry Into the Human Prospect* (New York 1974).

Chapter Seven
Representative Activities

This chapter is dedicated to Robert K. Merton 'with appreciation and affection'. It is part of a volume prepared in honour of Merton by T. Gieryn on behalf of the New York Academy of Sciences.

1 Merton, *Social Theory and Social Structure*, p. 532.
2 Eccles and Popper, *The Self and Its Brain*. Quotations from pp. 38, 39, 47.
3 Popper, *The Open Society and Its Enemies*, p. 277.
4 Cf. Hirsch, *Social Limits to Growth*.
5 A. Camus, *The Myth of Sisyphus* (Harmondsworth 1973), p. 92.
6 Josef König (1894–1975), Professor of Philosophy at Hamburg (1946–54) and Göttingen (since 1954), was the author of a treatise on the concept of intuition (*Der Begriff der Intuition*, 1926), and of one on the linguistic philosophy of being and thought (*Sein und Denken*, 1937).
7 Quotations from Aristotle, *Nicomachean Ethics*, X, 7.
8 F. Nietzsche, *Jenseits von Gut und Böse*, 126, and *Der Antichrist*, 4. My translation.
9 A. Camus, *The Myth of Sisyphus*, p. 192.
10 Cf. Bloch, *Zur Ontologie des Noch-Nicht-Seins*.
11 K. Marx, F. Engels, *Manifest der Kommunistischen Partei* (Berlin 1953), p. 19. My translation.
12 Cf. K. Mannheim, *Ideology and Utopia* (London 1936). In Chapter III Mannheim quotes A. Weber as the author of the term 'socially free-floating intelligentsia'.
13 Cf. M. Weber, 'Politik als Beruf', in *Politische Schriften*. Weber's terms are *Leidenschaft, Verantwortung, Augenmass*.
14 Cf. Arendt, *Vita Activa*.
15 Cf. M. Weber, 'Politik als Beruf', as well as the companion lecture on 'Wissenschaft als Beruf'.
16 O. Wälterlin, in *In Memoriam Max Reinhardt* (Zurich–New York 1944), p. 21.
17 K. Marx, *Thesen über Feuerbach*, Eleventh Thesis.
18 von Hayek, *The Constitution of Liberty*, p. 41.
19 Private communication from Sir Karl Popper.

[20] The Report by the Royal Commission on the Environment (under the chairmanship of Sir Brian Flowers) of 1977 provides an excellent example of such responsibility.

Index

Index of Subjects

Index of Names